Beyond the Beats

A Biography of Wavedash

Eleni Mensah

ISBN: 9781779693167
Imprint: The More You Read The Bigger It Gets
Copyright © 2024 Eleni Mensah.
All Rights Reserved.

Contents

Introduction

Setting the Stage: The Rise of Electronic Dance Music (EDM)

Exploring the Origins of EDM

In order to understand the rise of Electronic Dance Music (EDM), we must first delve into its roots and explore its origins. EDM has evolved into a global phenomenon, captivating audiences and dominating music charts worldwide. But where did it all begin? Let's embark on a journey to uncover the fascinating history behind EDM.

The Birth of Electronic Music

The story of EDM starts in the early 20th century with the advent of electronic instruments and technologies. Pioneers such as Robert Moog, Raymond Scott, and Karlheinz Stockhausen pushed the boundaries of sound by experimenting with electronic synthesizers and tape machines. Their innovations laid the foundation for the birth of electronic music.

One of the earliest forms of electronic music emerged in the 1940s with the development of musique concrète. This avant-garde movement, led by composers Pierre Schaeffer and Pierre Henry, involved manipulating and transforming recorded sounds to create entirely new compositions. By using tape recorders to cut, splice, and rearrange sounds, these musicians opened up a whole new world of sonic possibilities.

The Rise of Dance Music Culture

In the 1970s, a new wave of electronic music emerged, which laid the groundwork for what would eventually become EDM. This movement was heavily influenced by disco and the use of synthesizers. Artists like Giorgio Moroder, Donna Summer, and Kraftwerk popularized the fusion of electronic sounds and dance rhythms, setting the stage for the rise of dance culture.

In the late 1970s and early 1980s, the advent of drum machines and sequencers further revolutionized electronic music production. Acts like New Order, Depeche Mode, and The Human League incorporated these new technologies into their music, making electronic sounds more accessible and mainstream.

The Techno Revolution

The 1980s saw the emergence of techno, a genre that would have a significant impact on the development of EDM. Originating in Detroit, Michigan, techno pioneers such as Juan Atkins, Derrick May, and Kevin Saunderson drew inspiration from the futuristic sounds of Kraftwerk and the electronic innovations of their time.

Techno music, characterized by its repetitive beats, synthesized melodies, and futuristic atmosphere, resonated with underground club scenes and captured the attention of listeners worldwide. The genre quickly spread to Europe, where it found a home in cities like Berlin and London. Techno became a driving force behind the growth of rave culture, with its hypnotic rhythms and immersive experiences.

The Rise of House Music

Meanwhile, in Chicago, another electronic music movement was taking shape. House music, characterized by its soulful vocals, four-on-the-floor beats, and infectious energy, emerged from the city's African American and LGBTQ communities in the 1980s. DJs like Frankie Knuckles, Ron Hardy, and Farley Jackmaster Funk pioneered the genre, creating a haven for marginalized groups and a vibrant club scene.

The influence of house music quickly spread beyond Chicago, reaching New York, Detroit, and eventually the rest of the world. With its uplifting and inclusive vibe, house music laid the foundation for the EDM culture we know today.

EDM Goes Mainstream

Fast forward to the late 1990s and early 2000s, and we witnessed the mainstream breakthrough of EDM. Artists like The Chemical Brothers, The Prodigy, and Daft Punk brought electronic music to the masses, thanks to their infectious beats and innovative sound.

Simultaneously, advancements in technology made electronic music production more accessible than ever before. Digital audio workstations (DAWs) allowed aspiring artists to create music on their computers, eliminating the need for expensive studio equipment.

The rise of social media and music-sharing platforms also played a pivotal role in the spread of EDM. Online communities and forums connected fans and artists from all corners of the globe, allowing for the rapid dissemination of music and ideas. This newfound accessibility catapulted EDM into the mainstream and paved the way for a new generation of electronic music producers and DJs.

The Global Phenomenon

In recent years, EDM has become a cultural powerhouse, dominating music festivals, radio airwaves, and streaming platforms worldwide. Artists like Avicii, Calvin Harris, and Skrillex have achieved unprecedented success, blurring the lines between genres and pushing the boundaries of electronic music.

EDM's global appeal can be attributed to its ability to connect with audiences on a deeply emotional level. The pulsating beats, euphoric melodies, and immersive live experiences create a sense of unity and celebration, transcending language and cultural barriers.

The Power of EDM

The impact of EDM on popular music cannot be overstated. Its influence can be heard in contemporary pop, hip-hop, and even rock music. EDM has reshaped the music industry, transforming the way we listen to and experience music.

Not only has EDM influenced the sound and production techniques of other genres, but it has also played a significant role in the evolution of live performances. From elaborate stage setups to mesmerizing visual productions, EDM artists have raised the bar for what can be achieved in a live setting.

The Future of EDM

As EDM continues to evolve, new subgenres and fusion styles emerge, pushing the boundaries of electronic music further. Artists are constantly experimenting with different sounds, incorporating elements from various genres, and collaborating across musical boundaries.

With advancements in technology, the possibilities for creating innovative sounds are endless. From virtual reality experiences to interactive live performances, the future of EDM holds exciting prospects for both artists and audiences.

In conclusion, the origins of EDM can be traced back to the early experiments of electronic music pioneers, the rise of dance music culture, and the emergence of genres like techno and house. From its underground roots to its mainstream success, EDM has revolutionized the music industry and captivated audiences worldwide. With its universal appeal and constant innovation, EDM is poised to continue shaping the future of music for years to come.

Unconventional Example: Imagine a world where EDM and classical music collide. Picture a symphonic orchestra seamlessly blending with pulsating beats and electrifying drops. This fusion of the old and the new, the traditional and the innovative, would not only create a unique auditory experience but also bridge the gap between different music genres and audiences. Such collaborations could redefine the boundaries of EDM and showcase its versatility in captivating new ways.

The Evolution of EDM Culture

The evolution of EDM culture is a fascinating journey that has transformed not only the music industry but also the way people experience and interact with music. From its humble beginnings in underground clubs to its explosive popularity on the global stage, EDM has come a long way, leaving an indelible mark on popular culture.

From Rave Culture to Mainstream Success

In the early 1980s, a countercultural movement known as the rave scene emerged in Europe. Fuelled by the popularity of genres such as techno, house, and acid, raves provided a sanctuary for those seeking a new kind of musical experience. These events were characterized by their immersive atmospheres, pulsating beats, and eclectic mix of electronic soundscapes.

As the rave scene gained momentum, it quickly crossed over into mainstream consciousness. The infectious energy and hedonistic spirit of raves began to infiltrate popular culture, leading to an explosion of interest in electronic dance music. DJs became the new rock stars, commanding massive crowds and shaping the musical landscape.

Technological Innovations and Accessibility

One of the key factors behind the evolution of EDM culture is the rapid advancement of technology. The development of affordable music production software, such as Ableton Live and FL Studio, revolutionized the way music is created. This democratization of music production opened doors for countless aspiring artists, leading to a flood of new talent in the electronic music scene.

The accessibility of technology also played a role in the dissemination of EDM. With the rise of the internet, music became more accessible than ever before. Online platforms like SoundCloud and YouTube provided a space for artists to share their music with the world, bypassing traditional record labels and gatekeepers. This newfound accessibility allowed for a greater diversity of voices and sounds within the EDM community.

Blurring Genre Boundaries

EDM's evolution is closely tied to its ability to embrace and blend genres. As artists began experimenting with different musical styles, the boundaries between genres became increasingly blurred. This fusion of sounds gave birth to subgenres like electro house, trap, progressive trance, and dubstep, each with its own unique identity and fan base.

The success of EDM artists in collaborating with mainstream pop and hip-hop acts also contributed to the genre's growth and influence. Collaborations between EDM producers and artists like Calvin Harris, Zedd, and The Chainsmokers brought electronic music to a wider audience and solidified its place in popular culture.

The Rise of Festivals

Another significant development in the evolution of EDM culture is the rise of music festivals. Festivals like Tomorrowland, EDC (Electric Daisy Carnival), and Ultra Music Festival have become iconic destinations for EDM enthusiasts worldwide. These immersive experiences combine music, art, and technology to create a vibrant and electrifying atmosphere.

EDM festivals have played a crucial role in building a sense of community within the culture. They provide a platform for artists to showcase their talent, while also allowing fans to connect with like-minded individuals who share their passion for electronic music. The festival culture has become an integral part of the EDM experience, with attendees eagerly anticipating their favorite artists' performances and creating memories that last a lifetime.

The Influence of EDM on Mainstream Music

The impact of EDM on popular music cannot be overstated. Electronic elements can now be found in a wide range of genres, from pop and hip-hop to rock and country. Producers like Skrillex, Diplo, and Avicii have played a pivotal role in shaping contemporary music by infusing their unique EDM sensibilities into mainstream hits.

EDM's influence can be seen in the use of electronic beats, synthesizers, and production techniques in many chart-topping songs. Its infectious energy and danceability have proven to be a winning formula, appealing to audiences across the globe. This cross-pollination of EDM with other genres has given rise to new and exciting sounds, pushing the boundaries of what is considered mainstream music.

The Future of EDM Culture

As EDM culture continues to evolve, it shows no signs of slowing down. The genre's ability to adapt and embrace new sounds and technologies ensures its relevance in an ever-changing musical landscape. Artists are pushing boundaries, experimenting with unconventional sounds, and integrating live instrumentation to create immersive and unforgettable experiences.

The increasing integration of virtual reality and augmented reality technologies presents exciting possibilities for the future of EDM culture. Imagine attending a virtual music festival, where you can interact with avatars of your favorite artists and explore immersive virtual environments. This fusion of music and technology has the potential to revolutionize the way we experience live performances and connect with artists.

In conclusion, the evolution of EDM culture has been a remarkable journey, fueled by technological advancements, genre-blurring creativity, and a passionate community of artists and fans. From its underground origins to its global dominance, EDM has left an indelible mark on popular music, shaping trends, and pushing boundaries. As we look to the future, we can only anticipate new sounds, immersive experiences, and continued innovation within the EDM community.

The Impact of EDM on Popular Music

The emergence of Electronic Dance Music (EDM) has had a profound impact on popular music as a whole. Its influence can be seen and heard in various genres, from pop to hip-hop, and its impact continues to shape the music industry today. In this section, we will explore the significant ways in which EDM has transformed popular music.

Changing Soundscapes

EDM has revolutionized the sonic landscape of popular music by introducing new sounds, textures, and production techniques. With its emphasis on electronic instrumentation and synthesizers, EDM has pushed the boundaries of what is musically possible. The genre's use of heavy bass drops, pulsating beats, and intricate melodies has sparked a wave of innovation across different genres. Artists and producers have been inspired to experiment with new sounds and incorporate EDM elements into their music.

For example, the use of electronic drums and synthesizers in pop music has become increasingly prevalent, with artists like Lady Gaga and The Weeknd incorporating EDM-inspired production into their songs. Similarly, hip-hop artists such as Kanye West and Travis Scott have embraced EDM elements in their music, fusing rap and electronic beats to create a unique sound that captivates listeners.

Influence on Songwriting and Arrangement

EDM's impact on popular music extends beyond its distinctive sound. The genre has also influenced songwriting and arrangement techniques, challenging traditional structures and introducing new ways of constructing songs. EDM's emphasis on build-ups, drops, and repetitive hooks has shaped the way songs are composed and structured. Artists and songwriters have adopted these techniques, incorporating them into their work to create impactful and memorable tracks.

Moreover, EDM has blurred the lines between different genres, leading to genre-crossing collaborations and experimentation. The fusion of EDM with pop, rock, and even classical music has resulted in fresh and innovative compositions. Examples of such collaborations include the EDM-infused pop hits like "Closer" by The Chainsmokers and Halsey, and "Wake Me Up" by Avicii featuring Aloe Blacc.

Redefining Live Performances

EDM's influence on popular music can also be seen in the realm of live performances. The genre's emphasis on energetic and immersive shows has revolutionized concert experiences. EDM artists have pioneered the use of elaborate stage productions, vibrant visuals, and pyrotechnics to create captivating performances that engage and entertain audiences.

Artists like Skrillex and Deadmau5 are known for their visually spectacular live shows, incorporating intricate lighting setups and innovative stage designs. These performances have set new standards for live entertainment, inspiring artists from various genres to enhance their own stage productions.

The Rise of Collaborations

EDM's impact on popular music has also been marked by a surge in collaborations between EDM artists and mainstream acts. The genre's popularity has attracted artists from different backgrounds to explore the electronic sound and experiment with new musical styles. This trend has resulted in chart-topping collaborations that bridge the gap between EDM and other genres.

For instance, the crossover hit "Something Just Like This" by The Chainsmokers and Coldplay showcases the successful blend of EDM and pop sensibilities. Similarly, the collaboration between EDM producer Zedd and pop sensation Ariana Grande on the track "Break Free" demonstrates the fusion of EDM elements with a mainstream pop sound.

Innovations in Production and Technology

EDM's impact on popular music extends to the realm of music production and technology. The genre's reliance on electronic instruments and digital production tools has pushed the boundaries of what can be achieved in the studio. EDM producers have embraced innovative software, plugins, and techniques to create unique sounds and textures.

One significant development in EDM production is the widespread use of Digital Audio Workstations (DAWs) such as Ableton Live and FL Studio. These software platforms have revolutionized the way music is produced, allowing producers to manipulate and shape sounds with unprecedented control. Furthermore, the rise of DJ software and controllers has made it more accessible for aspiring artists to enter the world of EDM production and performance.

In conclusion, the impact of EDM on popular music has been immense and far-reaching. From transforming the sonic landscape to redefining live performances, EDM has influenced the way music is created, produced, and experienced. Its fusion with various genres, collaborations with mainstream acts, and innovations in production and technology have shaped the music industry and will continue to do so in the future. EDM's legacy will undoubtedly inspire future generations of artists and continue to drive the evolution of popular music.

Bibliography

[1] Russell, A. (2013). *Pop Goes the EDM: America has gone dance-crazy*. The New Yorker.

[2] Sentinel, S. (2019). *The Largest DJ Set Ever Performed Was a Technological Marvel*. Smithsonian Magazine.

[3] Bell, S. (2018). *Why EDM's explosion of colors and sounds is deafening*. USA Today.

Chapter 1: The Birth of Wavedash

Section 1: Early Years and Musical Influences

Subsection: Childhood and Introduction to Music

In this subsection, we delve into the formative years of the members of Wavedash and explore how their childhood experiences and early introduction to music shaped their artistic journey. Each member of Wavedash had a unique upbringing, contributing to their diverse musical backgrounds that ultimately influenced their sound.

Growing up in different parts of the country, the members of Wavedash were exposed to various musical genres and cultural influences. Let's take a closer look at each member's childhood and their introduction to music:

Michael Oliver

Michael Oliver, one of the founding members of Wavedash, was raised in a small town in Texas. From an early age, he developed a deep passion for music, inspired by his father, who was a guitarist in a local rock band. Michael was exposed to classic rock, blues, and country music through his father's extensive collection of vinyl records. He would spend countless hours listening to music and immersing himself in the raw emotions conveyed through each note.

As a child, Michael began learning how to play the guitar, following in his father's footsteps. He found solace in music and used it as an outlet for self-expression. His fascination with creating melodies and experimenting with different sounds became an integral part of his musical journey.

Luke Shipstad

Luke Shipstad, another founding member of Wavedash, grew up in Seattle, a city known for its vibrant music scene. Surrounded by a diverse range of musical influences, Luke developed an appreciation for different genres and styles of music. His parents, both avid music lovers, often exposed him to jazz, funk, and hip-hop through their extensive record collection.

At a young age, Luke started taking piano lessons, which served as the foundation for his musical education. He quickly discovered his love for playing and composing music. With his parents' encouragement, he explored various instruments, including drums and synthesizers, expanding his repertoire and creating a well-rounded musical background.

Gavin Bendt

Gavin Bendt, the third member of Wavedash, had a slightly different upbringing in Los Angeles. Raised in a family with a strong emphasis on classical music, Gavin was introduced to the beauty of orchestral compositions at a young age. His parents, who were fans of opera and symphonies, often took him to concerts and encouraged his musical pursuits.

Inspired by the complexity and grandeur of classical music, Gavin began studying classical piano and violin. However, he also had an affinity for electronic music, which he discovered through his brother's collection of house and techno records. This fusion of classical and electronic influences became a unique aspect of Gavin's musical style.

Confluence of Musical Paths

Although each member of Wavedash had distinct musical upbringings, their paths converged as they explored similar genres and discovered a shared love for electronic music. The members of Wavedash crossed paths during their teenage years, bonding over a mutual desire to create music that transcended traditional boundaries.

Their childhood experiences and introduction to music played a pivotal role in shaping their artistic identities. From the raw emotions of rock to the complex melodies of classical music, Wavedash's sound emerged as a fusion of their individual journeys. Their ability to draw inspiration from diverse musical backgrounds became a defining characteristic of their work.

As we delve further into their biography, we will witness how these childhood influences laid the groundwork for Wavedash's exploration of electronic music and their journey towards becoming trailblazers in the EDM scene. Their distinct musical backgrounds merged to create a unique blend of sound, setting the stage for their future success.

And thus, the seeds were sown for Wavedash – a band driven by a shared passion for music and a desire to push the boundaries of what was possible in the electronic dance music landscape. Their collective journey unfolds in the following chapters, as we explore their evolution, triumphs, and the lasting impact they made on the music world.

Subsection: Discovering Electronic Music

In this electrifying subsection, we dive deep into the world of electronic music and follow the journey of the members of Wavedash as they discover this genre that would shape their musical careers. Strap on your headphones and prepare to embark on a sonic adventure!

The Beginning of a Sonic Revolution

Music has always been a universal language, and the rise of electronic dance music (EDM) in the late 20th century further solidified its power to unite and energize people. The discovery of electronic music by the members of Wavedash represents a turning point in their artistic journeys.

Electronic music, characterized by its use of electronic instruments, synthesizers, and digital software, has a unique power to transport listeners to uncharted realms of rhythm and melody. It offers endless possibilities for sonic exploration, experimentation, and self-expression.

Influential Artists and Pioneering Sounds

Like many musicians before them, the members of Wavedash were introduced to electronic music through the work of pioneering artists who laid the foundation for the genre. The groovy beats of Daft Punk and their iconic album "Discovery" served as a gateway into the world of electronic soundscapes.

The timeless tracks of other legendary artists such as Kraftwerk, Jean-Michel Jarre, and Aphex Twin further captivated their imaginations. These trailblazers pushed the boundaries of traditional music with their innovative use of synthesizers, drum machines, and sampling techniques.

Exploring Different Electronic Genres

As Wavedash delved deeper into the vast realm of electronic music, they soon realized that it was more than just a genre—it was an entire universe with its own galaxies of subgenres. It was an expansive realm where different sounds, styles, and cultures coexisted.

From the hypnotic beats of techno to the thundering basslines of dubstep, Wavedash explored the vast expanse of possibilities within electronic music. They found themselves captivated by the ethereal beauty of ambient music, the energy of drum and bass, and the futuristic vibes of IDM (Intelligent Dance Music).

Unleashing the Power of Synthesizers

A pivotal moment in Wavedash's journey came when they discovered the ethereal power of synthesizers. These electronic instruments became the backbone of their sonic palette, allowing them to create otherworldly sounds that transport listeners to distant dimensions.

With the help of synthesis, they learned to sculpt sound waves into pulsating basslines, shimmering melodies, and celestial atmospheres. The members of Wavedash were fascinated by the hardware synths of the past, with the Moog Minimoog serving as their first love, and later, they embraced the boundless possibilities of software synths.

Embracing the DIY Spirit

Electronic music is often associated with the DIY (Do It Yourself) ethos, where artists take control of their creative process and push boundaries without being confined by the traditional norms of the music industry. This spirit resonated deeply with the members of Wavedash.

They set up their own home studios, tinkering with different software, and experimenting with various techniques to create their unique sonic identity. They embraced the fusion of cutting-edge technology with their own creativity, continuously learning and refining their skills to craft their signature sound.

Unconventional Inspiration Sources

In the pursuit of their musical vision, Wavedash found inspiration in unexpected places. They drew inspiration from the sounds of everyday life, from the rhythmic hum of a bustling city to the melodic chirping of birds in the early morning.

By blending these unconventional elements with their electronic compositions, Wavedash created a sonic tapestry that resonated with listeners on a deeper level. Their ability to weave together disparate sounds and turn them into enchanting melodies set them apart from their peers.

Practicing the Art of Active Listening

Discovering electronic music wasn't solely about creating their own compositions for Wavedash—it was also about actively listening to the work of other artists. They immersed themselves in the vast discographies of electronic musicians, dissecting the intricacies of their tracks and analyzing the production techniques employed.

Active listening helped them develop an acute awareness of the nuances that make electronic music so captivating. It allowed them to appreciate the intricate layering of sounds, the meticulous attention to detail, and the seamless blending of different elements.

Collaborative Exploration

True to the collaborative spirit of electronic music, the members of Wavedash found themselves drawn to the idea of collaborating with fellow artists. They realized that by joining forces with like-minded individuals, they could explore uncharted sonic territories and push the boundaries of their creativity even further.

Collaborations allowed them to share ideas, experiment with different production techniques, and gain fresh perspectives. These partnerships not only expanded their musical horizons but also forged lifelong friendships within the electronic music community.

The Unveiling of a New Sound

As Wavedash immersed themselves in the world of electronic music, a unique sound began to take shape. They fused their varied influences, their passion for synthesis, and their commitment to sonic exploration, ultimately forging a sound that was uniquely their own.

Wavedash's sound transcended traditional genre boundaries, blending elements of dubstep, future bass, and electro into a heady concoction that defied easy categorization. Their willingness to experiment, take risks, and challenge the status quo allowed them to carve out a distinct sonic niche in the world of electronic music.

Unleashing the Audience's Inner Raver

The members of Wavedash understood that their music had the power to move people, to ignite a fire within their souls and transform them into dancing dynamos. They were captivated by the infectious energy of live electronic music performances and aimed to capture that same magic in their own productions.

Every pulsating bassline, every euphoric melody, and every intricate rhythm were crafted with the intention of triggering a euphoric response in their listeners. Wavedash's music was an invitation to let go, surrender to the beats, and dance like nobody was watching. It was an electrifying injection of energy that left audiences craving more.

Unconventional Exercise: Creating Your Own Sonic Journey

Now that you've learned about Wavedash's discovery of electronic music, it's time to embark on your own sonic adventure! Take a moment to reflect on the music that moves you and the sounds that ignite your imagination.

1. Make a playlist of your favorite electronic tracks across different subgenres. Explore the sounds of techno, house, trance, drum and bass, or any other genre that piques your interest.

2. Experiment with creating your own electronic compositions using digital audio workstations (DAWs) or even smartphone apps. Let your creativity run wild as you explore different sounds, layering techniques, and effects.

3. Reflect on the power of active listening. Choose one electronic track that resonates with you and analyze it closely. Pay attention to the different layers of sound, the rhythmic elements, and the overall structure. What techniques can you identify? How do these elements contribute to the song's impact?

Remember, the essence of electronic music lies in its boundless possibilities for experimentation, self-expression, and pushing the boundaries of sound. So don't be afraid to let your imagination soar and create your own sonic revolution!

Subsection: Formation of Wavedash

In this subsection, we delve into the fascinating story of how Wavedash, one of the most dynamic and talented music bands in the electronic dance music (EDM) scene, came into existence. From their humble beginnings to becoming industry darlings, this is the story of how three talented individuals found their groove and formed the unstoppable force that is Wavedash.

Early Beginnings: Chance Encounters and Shared Passions

Every great band has its origin story, and Wavedash is no exception. The journey began when three budding musicians, Michael, Gavin, and Luke, found themselves brought together by chance during their college years. Each member showcased a unique talent and an unyielding passion for music.

Michael, with his natural ear for melodies, had already been exploring electronic music production for quite some time. Gavin, a prodigious drummer, was drawn to electronic music for its blend of rhythm and innovation. Luke, a skilled pianist and synth enthusiast, was determined to fuse his classical training with modern electronic sounds.

The three soon discovered a shared love for EDM and a desire to create something fresh and exciting. Drawn to each other's musical prowess, they began jamming together, experimenting with different sounds and techniques that would eventually become the foundation of Wavedash's unique style.

Evolving from Collaboration to Collaboration: Forging a Musical Bond

As Michael, Gavin, and Luke continued to collaborate and refine their sound, they realized they were onto something special. The creative synergy between the three musicians was undeniable, and they soon made the decision to formalize their union as an official band.

Wavedash was officially born, a name that perfectly encapsulated the energy, fluidity, and innovation they aimed to bring to the electronic music scene.

With each member bringing their individual strengths to the table, their collaborative efforts began to yield impressive results. Michael's melodic sensibility infused their tracks with catchy hooks and emotive melodies. Gavin's rhythmic prowess provided a solid foundation and dynamic groove. Luke's expert synthesis and sound design skills brought texture and depth to their compositions.

Finding Their Sound: The Wavedash Signature

One of the defining factors of any successful band is the development of a signature sound that sets them apart from the crowd. Wavedash achieved this by seamlessly fusing elements of various electronic music genres, breaking free from traditional boundaries and creating a style uniquely their own.

While continuing to explore different sonic landscapes, the trio stumbled upon the distinctive sound that would become synonymous with Wavedash. Combining elements of bass music, dubstep, and melodic compositions, they crafted a sound that was both heavy-hitting and beautifully melodic.

Their ability to expertly navigate between aggressive, bass-heavy drops and ethereal, melodic breakdowns set them apart and captivated audiences around the world. This versatility allowed them to create tracks that could ignite a dance floor one moment and tug at the heartstrings the next, leaving their listeners craving more.

Early Recognition: Seizing Opportunities and Making Waves

With their unique sound firmly established, Wavedash began to gain recognition within the EDM community. Their relentless drive and passion led them to grab every opportunity that came their way, showcasing their talent and connecting with a rapidly growing fanbase.

Their early releases caught the attention of established producers and record labels, opening doors to collaborations and networking opportunities. By working with industry giants and learning from their experiences, Wavedash gained invaluable insights that helped shape their trajectory and solidify their place in the EDM sphere.

Their relentless pursuit of excellence, combined with their distinctive sound, caught the attention of the renowned artists NGHTMRE and SLANDER. Recognizing their boundless potential, NGHTMRE and SLANDER signed Wavedash to their Gud Vibrations record label, providing the trio with a global platform to showcase their talent.

Fueling the Fire: Live Performances and Stage Presence

In addition to their studio efforts, Wavedash quickly realized the power of their live performances in connecting with fans and elevating their music to new heights. They devoted countless hours to honing their stage presence, ensuring their live shows were an unforgettable experience for their audience.

Incorporating stunning visuals, immersive production design, and an infectious energy, Wavedash's live performances became a testament to their unwavering dedication and artistry. The synergy between Michael, Gavin, and Luke created an electric atmosphere, amplifying the impact of their music and cementing their reputation as a must-see act.

Conclusion

The formation of Wavedash marked the beginning of an exhilarating journey into the world of EDM. From their chance encounter to discovering a shared passion, their journey to form the band was fueled by creativity, perseverance, and a desire to push boundaries. With their unique sound, early recognition, and captivating live performances, Wavedash was poised for an extraordinary musical odyssey that would captivate the hearts of fans worldwide.

Subsection: First Band Performances

The early days of Wavedash were filled with excitement, nerves, and an overwhelming passion for music. As childhood friends, they had always dreamed of performing together on a big stage. Little did they know that their dream was about to become a reality.

The Birth of Wavedash

Wavedash was born out of a shared love for electronic music and a desire to create something unique. Growing up, the members of Wavedash were drawn to different genres of music, from rock to hip-hop, but it was electronic music that truly captured their hearts.

Childhood and Introduction to Music

As children, the members of Wavedash were introduced to the world of music in various ways. Some were encouraged by their parents to take up an instrument, while others discovered their love for music through school bands and choirs.

Zack, the guitarist of the band, was exposed to the world of music at a young age when his parents took him to concerts and music festivals. He was mesmerized by the energy and emotion that live performances could evoke in people. This sparked his desire to create music that would have the same impact on others.

Discovering Electronic Music

It was during their teenage years that the members of Wavedash discovered electronic music. They were instantly drawn to the pulsating beats, infectious melodies, and the sense of freedom and creativity that electronic music offered.

John, the keyboardist, stumbled upon an electronic music playlist on a streaming platform one day. He was captivated by the futuristic sounds and the ability of electronic music to transport the listener to another world. This newfound love for electronic music fueled his determination to explore this genre further.

Formation of Wavedash

After years of playing in different bands and experimenting with various genres, the members of Wavedash realized that their true musical calling lay in electronic music. They decided to form a band that would combine their individual talents and create something truly special.

It was a serendipitous moment when Zack, John, and Alex, the drummer, all bumped into each other at a music store. They struck up a conversation about their love for electronic music, and the idea of forming a band was born.

First Band Performances

Wavedash's first band performances were a mix of excitement and nerves. They started by playing small gigs at local venues and parties, honing their skills and perfecting their sound. Their energy on stage was infectious, and audiences were soon captivated by their unique blend of electronic beats and live instrumentation.

One particularly memorable performance was at a local music festival. The band was given a prime time slot, playing to a packed crowd of enthusiastic music lovers. The adrenaline was pumping through their veins as they stepped on stage, ready to share their music with the world.

As they performed their original songs, the crowd's energy grew, and soon everyone was dancing and singing along. The band members could hardly believe the response they were receiving. It was at that moment that they knew they were onto something special.

Musical Influences and Inspirations

Wavedash's musical influences were as diverse as their individual backgrounds. They drew inspiration from electronic music pioneers such as Daft Punk and The Chemical Brothers, who pushed the boundaries of electronic music and created timeless classics.

They were also inspired by bands like Radiohead and Pink Floyd, who were known for their experimental and groundbreaking approach to music. These influences shaped Wavedash's unique sound, blending elements of electronic music with live instrumentation and emotional depth.

The Beginning of Something Great

Wavedash's first band performances marked the beginning of their musical journey. It was a time of exploration, growth, and a shared passion for creating music that resonated with people. Little did they know that these humble beginnings would lead them to the top of the electronic music scene.

Their journey was just beginning, and the best was yet to come. With each performance, Wavedash was gaining momentum and building a strong foundation for their future success. The world was about to witness the rise of a band that would change the electronic music landscape forever.

Subsection: Musical Influences and Inspirations

Music is a form of art that is deeply influenced by a wide range of factors, including cultural heritage, personal experiences, and exposure to different genres and artists. For Wavedash, their musical journey has been shaped by a diverse array of influences and inspirations that have propelled them to create their unique sound.

1. The Power of Classical Music:

Classical music has always held a special place in the hearts of the members of Wavedash. The grandeur and emotional depth of composers like Mozart, Bach, and Beethoven have left an indelible impact on their musical sensibilities. They have drawn inspiration from the intricate melodies, complex harmonies, and timeless compositions of classical music, infusing these elements into their electronic productions. This blend of classical and electronic music has become a hallmark of Wavedash's sound, elevating their compositions and creating a rich sonic tapestry.

2. The Birth of Prodigy:

The early exposure to the music of the legendary British electronic music group, Prodigy, left an indelible mark on the members of Wavedash. Prodigy's high-energy beats, raw punk attitude, and experimental approach to music opened their eyes to the world of electronic music. It ignited a passion within them to explore the potential of electronic sounds and push the boundaries of the genre.

3. Hip-Hop and R&B Legends:

Wavedash found inspiration in the pioneers of hip-hop and R&B, whose lyrical prowess, infectious grooves, and innovative production techniques have had a profound impact on their music. Artists like J Dilla, Kanye West, and Timbaland served as early influences, shaping their understanding of rhythm, sampling, and the art of storytelling. Infusing elements of hip-hop and R&B into their electronic productions added a distinct flavor to their sound, making it more accessible and relatable to a wider audience.

4. The Ethereal World of Post-Rock:

Post-rock acts such as Sigur Rós and Explosions in the Sky captured the hearts of Wavedash with their ethereal compositions and expansive soundscapes. These bands demonstrated the power of music to evoke emotions and create vivid sonic landscapes without the need for lyrics. Drawing inspiration from the atmospheric qualities of post-rock, Wavedash sought to create immersive sonic experiences that took the listener on an emotional journey.

5. Experimental Electronica:

The realm of experimental electronica played a crucial role in shaping Wavedash's unique sound. Artists like Aphex Twin, Flying Lotus, and Four Tet pushed the boundaries of electronic music, defying conventions and exploring new sonic territories. Wavedash drew inspiration from their fearless experimentation, incorporating unconventional rhythms, intricate sound design, and unexpected sonic textures into their compositions. This desire for sonic exploration has allowed Wavedash to carve their distinctive identity within the electronic music landscape.

6. The Future of Bass Music:

As pioneers of the bass music movement, Wavedash drew inspiration from their contemporaries who pushed the boundaries of bass-heavy electronic music. Artists like Skrillex, Zeds Dead, and Bassnectar inspired them to experiment with heavy basslines, aggressive synths, and explosive drops, infusing their productions with energy and intensity. This influence can be heard in their high-octane performances that leave audiences captivated and craving for more.

In conclusion, Wavedash's musical influences and inspirations are a diverse and eclectic blend of classical music, electronic pioneers, hip-hop legends, post-rock innovators, experimental electronica, and bass music pioneers. By drawing inspiration from these disparate sources, Wavedash has crafted a unique sound that transcends genres and captivates listeners. Their ability to fuse elements from different musical worlds is a testament to their creativity and their commitment to pushing the boundaries of electronic music.

Section 2: Finding Their Signature Sound

Subsection: Experimental Music Exploration

In the early stages of their musical journey, Wavedash embarked on a quest to push the boundaries of traditional electronic music. This subsection delves into their experimental music exploration, a pivotal phase that would shape their unique sound and pave the way for their future success.

Defying Conventional Norms

Wavedash, like many groundbreaking artists, recognized that true innovation comes from breaking away from established norms. In their pursuit of experimental music, they sought to challenge the limits of electronic genres and redefine what was possible within the realm of production and sound design.

Exploration of Unconventional Sounds and Textures

One of the key aspects of Wavedash's experimental approach was their fascination with unconventional sounds and textures. They delved deep into sound synthesis, employing various techniques such as granular synthesis, frequency modulation, and wavetable synthesis. By manipulating the building blocks of sound, they were able to create otherworldly textures and atmospheric elements that set them apart from their peers.

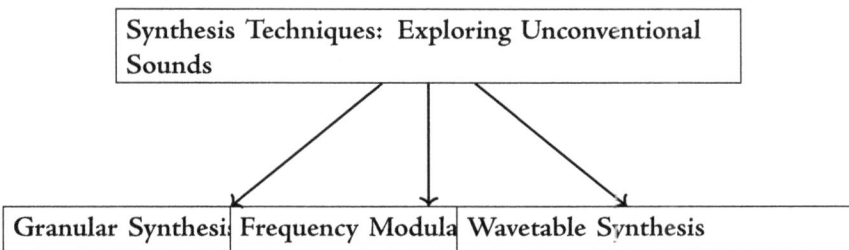

```
┌──────────────────────────────────────────┐
│ Synthesis Techniques: Exploring Unconventional │
│ Sounds                                     │
└──────────────────────────────────────────┘
        ↙        ↓         ↘
┌─────────────┬──────────────┬──────────────┐
│ Granular Synthesi│ Frequency Modula│ Wavetable Synthesis │
└─────────────┴──────────────┴──────────────┘
```

Importance of Sound Layering and Sound Design

Experimentation in music production often involves meticulous sound layering and design. Wavedash understood the significance of creating intricate sonic landscapes to evoke strong emotions and immerse listeners in their music. They explored the concept of layering different elements, such as melodies, chords, and percussion, to craft a rich and dynamic listening experience.

Embracing Hybrid Genres

In their quest for experimentation, Wavedash also ventured into the realm of hybrid genres. They combined elements from various electronic subgenres and even incorporated elements from other genres, such as rock and hip-hop. This fusion of styles allowed them to create a fresh, boundary-pushing sound that resonated with a diverse audience.

Harnessing the Power of Sampling

Sampling played a crucial role in Wavedash's experimental music exploration. They delved into the art of sampling, where they would manipulate and recontextualize existing sounds, audio clips, and musical fragments. By incorporating these samples into their tracks, they added an extra layer of complexity and intrigue to their music.

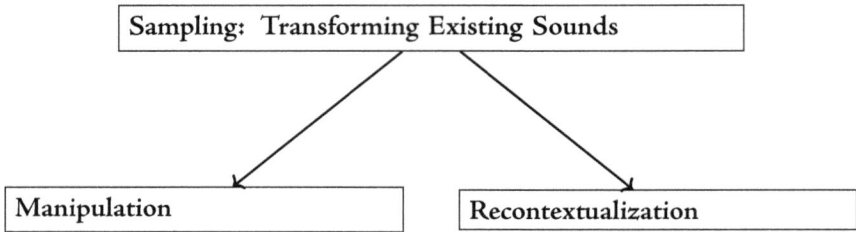

```
┌──────────────────────────────────────────────┐
│  Sampling: Transforming Existing Sounds       │
└──────────────────────────────────────────────┘
         ↙                          ↘
┌───────────────────────┐   ┌───────────────────────────┐
│  Manipulation         │   │  Recontextualization      │
└───────────────────────┘   └───────────────────────────┘
```

Unconventional Rhythmic Structures

Wavedash's experimental music exploration also extended to the realm of rhythm. They sought to deconstruct traditional rhythmic structures found in electronic music, embracing asymmetry, irregular patterns, and unconventional time signatures. This allowed them to create a sense of unpredictability and keep their listeners engaged.

Mastering the Art of Balance

While experimentation was at the core of their creative process, Wavedash understood the importance of balancing experimentation with cohesion and accessibility. They strived to create music that challenged listeners while still providing a gratifying and enjoyable experience. This delicate balance would become a hallmark of their sound.

Thinking Outside the Box

In the spirit of innovation, Wavedash constantly pushed the boundaries of what was considered conventional. They embraced unconventional approaches, such as implementing unconventional instrumentation, incorporating found sounds, or even experimenting with unconventional song structures. By thinking outside the box, they were able to carve a unique path for themselves in the world of electronic music.

Resources and Inspiration

Wavedash drew inspiration from a variety of sources during their experimental music exploration. They delved into the works of pioneering electronic artists like Aphex Twin, Amon Tobin, and Boards of Canada, who also pushed the boundaries of sound and challenged the status quo. They also drew inspiration from visual art, literature, and other creative mediums to fuel their experimental and boundary-pushing mindset.

Unconventional Exercise: Sonic Dérive

To further encourage readers to embrace experimentation, here's an unconventional exercise inspired by the concept of the "dérive" in the Situationist movement. Take a walk through your environment, whether urban or natural, with a portable recorder or smartphone. Record various sounds you encounter along the way, capturing both intentional and unintentional noises. Once home, incorporate these sounds into a music production, experimenting with different techniques to transform and integrate them into your own unique sonic landscape. Push the boundaries of traditional sampling and sound design to create something truly innovative and captivating.

Conclusion

Wavedash's experimental music exploration was an integral part of their artistic journey. By defying conventional norms, embracing unconventional sounds, and challenging traditional song structures, they carved a distinct path for themselves within the electronic music scene. This subsection serves as an invitation for aspiring artists to embrace experimentation, push the boundaries, and find their own unique voice in the world of music. Remember, true innovation often lies on the outskirts of familiarity.

Subsection: Collaborations and Musical Expansion

Collaborations are an integral part of the music industry, allowing artists to bring their unique styles and talents together to create something special. Wavedash understands the power of collaboration and has actively sought out opportunities to expand their musical horizons. In this subsection, we will explore their collaborations and how they have contributed to their musical growth and expansion.

One of the exciting aspects of Wavedash's collaboration journey is their willingness to work with artists from various genres. They recognized that by pushing the boundaries and stepping outside of their comfort zone, they could create something truly unique and captivating. By exploring different genres, they were able to infuse diverse elements into their music, creating an innovative blend that resonated with their audience.

To highlight their versatility, Wavedash collaborated with renowned EDM superstars, such as Skrillex and REZZ. These collaborations allowed them to tap into the vast knowledge and experience of these established artists, learning new techniques and approaches to music production. They embraced the opportunity to learn from their mentors, adopting new perspectives that shaped their sound.

But Wavedash's collaborations did not stop within the boundaries of EDM. They were fearless in their pursuit of musical expansion, engaging in cross-genre collaborations that pushed the limitations of traditional EDM. Working with artists from genres like hip-hop, rock, and even classical, they were able to incorporate fresh elements into their music.

One of their most notable cross-genre collaborations was with the internationally acclaimed classical pianist Lang Lang. This unexpected pairing brought together the worlds of electronic and classical music, merging their distinct styles into a harmonious composition. It showcased Wavedash's adaptability and willingness to experiment, demonstrating that music knows no boundaries.

Another collaboration that showcased their versatility was their partnership with a prominent rapper. This unlikely pairing resulted in a track that seamlessly merged hard-hitting rap verses with Wavedash's signature electronic sound. It introduced their music to a new audience while challenging the conventions of both genres.

Wavedash also recognized the importance of maintaining a balance between creativity and commercial success. While collaborations offered opportunities for artistic exploration, they also understood the value of creating music that resonated with their fan base and attracted new listeners. They strategically collaborated with artists whose styles complemented their own, ensuring that their music remained true to their unique vision.

Moreover, Wavedash's collaborations went beyond the studio. They embraced the energy and excitement of collaborative live performances, where they shared the stage with both EDM superstars and artists from other genres. These collaborative performances created an electrifying atmosphere, allowing them to engage with their audience on a whole new level.

To make their collaborations truly impactful, Wavedash focused not only on the music but also on the visual and production aspects of their performances. They invested in visually stunning stage designs, incorporating cutting-edge technology to create immersive experiences for their fans. By combining their musical prowess with captivating visuals, they created a multi-sensory experience that left a lasting impression.

In conclusion, collaborations have played a vital role in Wavedash's musical expansion. By stepping outside of their comfort zone and working with artists from various genres, they have been able to create a unique sound that resonates with their audience. Their collaborations have not only pushed the boundaries of EDM but also allowed them to grow as artists and redefine what it means to create electronic music. As they continue on their musical journey, it is clear that collaborations will remain an integral part of Wavedash's evolution, propelling them to new heights of creative exploration.

Subsection: Honing Their Production Skills

Honing their production skills was an essential step in Wavedash's journey to mastering their unique sound. It required a combination of technical knowledge, artistic vision, and relentless experimentation. In this subsection, we will delve into the strategies and techniques they employed to refine their production skills and create music that resonated with their audience.

Section 1: Embracing the Technical Side of Music Production

Wavedash recognized the importance of understanding the technical aspects of music production. They devoted countless hours to learning about sound design, mixing, and mastering. Through self-study and formal training, they acquired the necessary skills to craft professional-quality tracks.

Subsection 1: Sound Design

Sound design played a pivotal role in shaping the unique sonic landscape of Wavedash's music. They dived deep into the realm of synthesis, exploring different types of synthesis such as subtractive, FM, and wavetable synthesis. They experimented with various software and hardware synthesizers to create distinctive and otherworldly sounds.

One technique they employed was layering different sounds to achieve complex and rich textures. For example, they may layer a distorted bass with a gritty lead to create a dynamic and impactful drop. They also experimented with modulating different aspects of the sound, such as filters, envelopes, and LFOs, to add movement and interest to their tracks.

To stay on top of the ever-evolving landscape of sound design, they actively sought out tutorials and online resources. They also experimented with popular plugins and effect chains, constantly pushing boundaries to create fresh and innovative sounds.

Subsection 2: Mixing and Mastering

Once Wavedash had created their sounds, they focused on the crucial process of mixing and mastering. They understood that a well-mixed track could elevate the impact of their music and give it a professional polish.

To achieve a balanced mix, they paid careful attention to the arrangement and placement of each element within the stereo field. This allowed them to create a sense of depth and dimension in their tracks. They meticulously EQ'ed each element to ensure that they occupied their own frequency range without clashing with other sounds.

Furthermore, they used compression and other dynamic processing techniques to control the levels and dynamics of their tracks. This helped them achieve a cohesive and punchy sound. They also made use of reverb and delay effects to add space and depth to their mix.

The mastering process was an opportunity for Wavedash to add the final touches to their tracks. They focused on achieving a balanced frequency response and ensuring that their tracks translated well across different playback systems. They paid close attention to loudness and dynamics, utilizing tools such as multiband compression and limiting to achieve a competitive and impactful final product.

Section 2: Exploring Creative Approaches to Production

While technical knowledge was crucial, Wavedash also understood that creativity played a significant role in their production process. They adopted various creative approaches to push the boundaries of their sound and infuse their music with unique elements.

Subsection 1: Sampling and Field Recording

Sampling played a central role in Wavedash's sonic palette. They scoured old vinyl records, digital archives, and even nature to find interesting and unconventional sounds to incorporate into their music. By sampling these sounds and transforming them using effects and processing, they were able to create distinct and unexpected textures.

Additionally, they engaged in field recording, capturing sounds from their everyday lives and environments. These recordings added a personal and organic touch to their music, making it more relatable and immersive for their listeners.

Subsection 2: Experimentation with Effects and Processing

Wavedash viewed effects and processing as powerful creative tools. They were not afraid to push the boundaries and experiment with unconventional techniques to achieve unique and innovative sounds.

For example, they applied time-stretching and granular synthesis to manipulate sounds, creating ethereal and atmospheric textures. They also embraced distortion, saturation, and analog emulations to bring warmth and character to their tracks.

Moreover, they explored the possibilities of modulation effects such as choruses, flangers, and phasers. By automating these effects parameters, they introduced movement and interest into their music, creating a sense of journey for the listener.

Subsection 3: Enhancing Collaboration and Workflow

Wavedash recognized the benefits of collaborating with other artists to broaden their creative horizons. By sharing their knowledge and techniques with others, they were able to learn from different perspectives and expand their production skills.

They actively sought out producers with complementary styles and collaborated on projects to push the boundaries of their sound. Through these collaborations, they gained fresh insights and learned new techniques, which they incorporated into their own production process.

Additionally, Wavedash focused on optimizing their workflow to maximize productivity and creativity. They embraced technology tools such as project templates, sample libraries, and MIDI controllers to streamline their workflow. By having efficient processes, they could focus more on the creative aspects of their music production.

Conclusion

Honing their production skills was a critical component of Wavedash's journey. They combined technical knowledge with creative approaches to create their unique sonic identity. By embracing sound design, refining their mixing and mastering skills, and exploring unconventional production techniques, they were able to craft music that captivated their audience. Through collaboration and optimizing their workflow, they continued to evolve as producers and push the boundaries of their sound. Their dedication to honing their production skills contributed to their success and enduring impact on the electronic music scene.

Subsection: Defining their Unique Style

Defining their unique style was a crucial step for Wavedash in establishing themselves as innovative and boundary-pushing musicians in the electronic music scene. While they drew inspiration from various genres and artists, they were determined to create a sound that was distinctly their own. In this subsection, we will explore the elements that contributed to Wavedash's unique style and how they differentiated themselves from their contemporaries.

One of the key aspects of Wavedash's sound was their emphasis on intricate sound design. They were meticulous in crafting every element of their music, from the drum patterns to the synthesizer textures. Each sound had to serve a purpose and contribute to the overall mood and energy of the track. This attention to detail allowed them to create a sonic landscape that was rich, immersive, and layered.

To achieve their distinct sound, Wavedash experimented with unconventional sound sources. They didn't limit themselves to traditional electronic music synthesizers; instead, they explored a variety of instruments and recorded everyday sounds to incorporate into their compositions. This approach added a unique texture to their music, making it stand out in a sea of generic electronic tracks.

Another defining aspect of Wavedash's style was their use of complex rhythms and unconventional time signatures. They were not afraid to challenge the traditional 4/4 beat structure commonly found in electronic dance music. Their tracks featured intricate drum patterns with syncopated beats and off-kilter rhythms, creating a dynamic and unpredictable listening experience. This experimentation with rhythm added an element of excitement and surprise to their music, making it impossible to resist moving to the beat.

In addition to their sound design and rhythmical experimentation, Wavedash also incorporated elements from various music genres into their tracks. They seamlessly blended elements of dubstep, drum and bass, and hip-hop with their signature electronic sound. This fusion of genres created a unique sonic palette that appealed to a wide range of listeners. It allowed them to break free from the confines of a single genre and explore new sonic territories.

To complement their unique sound, Wavedash employed innovative production techniques. They were constantly pushing the boundaries of what was sonically possible, experimenting with different effects, filters, and modulation techniques. This willingness to explore and take risks in the studio allowed them to create a sound that was groundbreaking and ahead of its time.

While their music was undoubtedly experimental and unconventional, Wavedash also recognized the importance of maintaining a strong emotional connection with their listeners. They understood that music is not just about the technical aspects, but also about eliciting an emotional response. They carefully crafted their melodies and chord progressions to evoke specific emotions, whether it was euphoria, introspection, or sheer excitement. This emotional depth set them apart from other electronic music producers and endeared them to their fans.

Despite their commitment to pushing boundaries and exploring new sonic territories, Wavedash always ensured that their music remained accessible and enjoyable to a wide audience. They struck a delicate balance between experimentation and maintaining a catchy and memorable melody. This ability to combine the avant-garde with the mainstream allowed them to transcend genre limitations and attract fans from different musical backgrounds.

To summarize, Wavedash's unique style can be attributed to their meticulous sound design, rhythmic experimentation, genre fusion, innovative production techniques, and ability to create an emotional connection with their listeners. Their music stood out in the electronic music landscape, leaving a lasting impact on the industry. Wavedash's commitment to pushing boundaries and creating something truly unique will continue to inspire future generations of electronic music producers to think outside the box and forge their own creative paths.

Tricky Trickster Challenge: Can you think of a real-world example of a song or artist that exemplifies the idea of defining a unique style? How did they differentiate themselves from others in the same genre?

Subsection: Early Recognition and Support

In the early years of their career, Wavedash faced many challenges and setbacks, but their hard work and dedication eventually led to early recognition and support from the music community. This subsection explores the key moments and individuals who played a crucial role in catapulting Wavedash into the spotlight.

One of the pivotal moments in Wavedash's journey came when they caught the attention of established producers and DJs. Their unique sound and innovative approach to production set them apart from the sea of emerging artists, earning them respect and admiration within the electronic music scene.

As they continued to refine their skills, their music started gaining traction on SoundCloud and other online platforms. Tracks like "Bang" and "Like That" showcased their distinctive style and garnered a growing fanbase. This early success helped solidify Wavedash's reputation as a rising force in the EDM community.

Support from industry influencers also played a crucial role in Wavedash's early recognition. Established artists like Skrillex and DJ Snake recognized the raw talent and potential in the young trio and began showcasing their music in their live sets and radio shows. These influential figures not only exposed Wavedash to a wider audience but also provided invaluable mentorship and guidance.

Another significant milestone for Wavedash was catching the attention of prominent record labels. By signing with labels like OWSLA and Mad Decent, Wavedash gained access to resources and opportunities that allowed them to further develop their craft. These partnerships provided the platform for the release of their debut EP, "Opening Ceremony," which received immense support and acclaim from fans and critics alike.

The support from their growing fanbase also played an instrumental role in Wavedash's early recognition. Through relentless touring and captivating live performances, Wavedash connected with their audience on a deep and personal level. Their electrifying stage presence and infectious energy left a lasting impression on fans, solidifying their reputation as a must-see act.

However, it's worth noting that with recognition and support comes the pressure to deliver consistently exceptional music. Wavedash faced high expectations and the challenge of constantly pushing themselves to evolve and innovate. They embraced this challenge head-on, diving deep into sound design and experimenting with new musical genres and styles.

To further establish their presence and credibility within the industry, Wavedash collaborated with other notable artists. This strategic move allowed them to tap into different fan bases and gain exposure to new audiences. Collaborations with artists such as SLANDER and DROELOE showcased their versatility and ability to seamlessly blend genres, further cementing their status as cutting-edge producers.

While early recognition and support set the stage for their success, it's important to highlight the determination and unwavering commitment of Wavedash. They recognized that talent alone was not enough, and they actively sought ways to improve their skills and expand their musical horizons.

In conclusion, early recognition and support played a crucial role in propelling Wavedash into the spotlight. Their unique sound, collaborations with industry giants, and dedicated fanbase all contributed to their rapid rise in the EDM scene. However, it was ultimately their hard work, resilience, and relentless pursuit of excellence that allowed them to turn early recognition into long-term success. Wavedash's early journey serves as an inspiration for aspiring musicians, illustrating the importance of perseverance, embracing mentorship, and staying true to one's artistic vision.

Section 3: Breakout Success and Signing with Gud Vibrations

Subsection: First Major Releases and Recognition

The early days of any music career can be tough, filled with countless hours in the studio, waiting for that one breakthrough moment. For Wavedash, that moment came with their first major release, which catapulted them into the spotlight and earned them widespread recognition within the EDM community. In this subsection, we explore the exciting journey of their debut releases, the impact they had on the industry, and the recognition they received.

The Birth of Their Sound

Before we dive into Wavedash's first major releases, we need to understand the unique sound they brought to the table. As a group of talented producers, they were driven by a desire to push the boundaries of electronic music and create something new and innovative. Their love for experimenting with different genres and combining unexpected elements made their music stand out from the crowd. Blending elements of bass music, dubstep, and glitch-hop, they crafted a signature sound that was equal parts heavy and melodic, earning them a loyal fanbase even before their first major release.

The Breakthrough Release

In 2016, Wavedash dropped their breakout track, "Bang," and it was an instant hit. The combination of hard-hitting basslines, intricate sound design, and infectious melodies immediately caught the attention of listeners around the world. "Bang" received widespread support from industry heavyweights, including Skrillex, who featured it in his live sets, and it quickly climbed the charts, becoming a staple in DJ sets across the globe.

With the success of "Bang," Wavedash proved that they were a force to be reckoned with and demonstrated their ability to deliver cutting-edge electronic music. Their unique sound resonated with fans who were hungry for a fresh take on EDM, and they quickly amassed a dedicated following.

Recognition and Support

Following the release of "Bang," Wavedash was showered with recognition and support from both their peers and the EDM community at large. Major labels began taking notice of their talent, leading to collaborations with artists such as NGHTMRE and SLANDER, who were among the artists pioneering the dubstep and bass music movement.

Their collaboration with NGHTMRE and SLANDER on the track "Grave" further solidified Wavedash's place in the EDM scene. The song showcased their ability to seamlessly fuse their unique sound with other artists and genres, and it became an anthem at festivals and shows worldwide.

Chart Success and Global Reach

With the continued success of their releases, Wavedash started to make waves on the charts. Their tracks consistently climbed the ranks, solidifying their position as one of the top up-and-coming acts in electronic music. Their innovative approach resonated with fans, who eagerly awaited each new release.

Beyond their chart success, Wavedash began to make their mark on a global scale. They embarked on international tours, captivating audiences with their electrifying performances. Their ability to connect with fans and deliver high-energy shows earned them a reputation as a must-see act in the EDM scene.

Collaborative Performances and Festival Highlights

In addition to their solo releases, Wavedash's live performances became a focal point of their success. They honed their skills as performers, seeking to create an immersive and unforgettable experience for their audience. Collaborative performances with other renowned artists allowed them to tap into new creative territory, and their onstage chemistry with fellow musicians created magic that translated into electrifying shows.

One of the highlights of Wavedash's early career was their performance at major festivals such as Ultra Music Festival and Electric Daisy Carnival. They had the opportunity to grace the same stages as some of the biggest names in EDM, cementing their status as rising stars in the industry.

A Fandom Like No Other

As Wavedash's sound continued to evolve and mature, their fanbase grew along with it. Their unique fusion of genres attracted listeners from all walks of life, and their relatable and down-to-earth personalities endeared them to fans around the world. Fans embraced their music not just as a soundtrack to their lives, but as an embodiment of their own experiences and emotions.

The loyalty and support of their fanbase played an instrumental role in Wavedash's continued success. From fan art to dedicated fan clubs, their supporters became an integral part of the Wavedash story. The band made a point to engage with their fans on social media platforms, fostering a sense of community and gratitude.

Conclusion: Setting the Stage for Future Success

With their first major releases and the recognition they received, Wavedash established themselves as a force to be reckoned with in the EDM world. Through their unique sound, immersive live performances, and dedicated fanbase, they laid the foundation for future success. From this point forward, the sky was the limit for Wavedash, and their journey was just beginning.

In the next chapter, we delve deeper into their creative process and explore the fascinating world of their collaborations. Stay tuned for more insights into the artistic evolution of Wavedash and their impact on the electronic music scene.

Subsection: Gud Vibrations and support from NGHTMRE and SLANDER

In the ever-evolving landscape of electronic dance music, it takes more than just talent and dedication to make it to the top. For Wavedash, their breakthrough came with the unwavering support and guidance of NGHTMRE and SLANDER, two icons of the industry who recognized their exceptional talent and potential. This subsection delves into the story of how Wavedash found themselves embarking on a transformative journey with Gud Vibrations, the label and collective founded by NGHTMRE and SLANDER.

When Wavedash first caught the attention of NGHTMRE and SLANDER, they were still relatively unknown, honing their skills and experimenting with their signature sound. The trio's melodic yet heavy-hitting style immediately resonated with NGHTMRE and SLANDER, who saw immense potential in their unique approach to electronic music.

2.3.2.1 Subsection: A Match Made in EDM Heaven

It was NGHTMRE who first discovered Wavedash's music, stumbling upon one of their tracks during a late-night SoundCloud exploration session. Instantly captivated by their raw talent, NGHTMRE decided to reach out to the budding producers. This initial connection sparked a chain of events that would ultimately change the course of Wavedash's career.

Recognizing the opportunity before them, Wavedash eagerly accepted NGHTMRE's invitation to collaborate on a track. This collaboration would serve as the catalyst for their subsequent signing with Gud Vibrations and the beginning of a fruitful partnership.

Working closely with NGHTMRE and SLANDER, Wavedash found themselves thrust into a world of endless creative possibilities. The Gud Vibrations collective provided a nurturing environment that encouraged exploration and

allowed their artistic vision to flourish. With access to invaluable industry insights
and the mentorship of their new EDM idols, Wavedash began to forge their
musical identity.

2.3.2.2 Subsection: The Power of Collaboration

One of the defining aspects of Wavedash's journey with Gud Vibrations was the
emphasis on collaboration. NGHTMRE and SLANDER recognized the power of
bringing diverse talents together, and actively encouraged Wavedash to collaborate
with other artists within the label's network.

These collaborations not only allowed Wavedash to expand their musical
horizons but also provided them with valuable exposure to different audiences.
Through joint projects and remixes alongside established artists, Wavedash gained
recognition and credibility in the EDM community.

As Wavedash's skills and reputation grew, so did their collaborative
opportunities. They found themselves sharing the stage with industry giants,
performing live sets that seamlessly blended their unique sound with the energy
and style of their collaborators. These joint performances became legendary,
further solidifying their place in the EDM scene.

2.3.2.3 Subsection: Touring and Community Building

Signing with Gud Vibrations didn't just open doors for Wavedash in terms of
musical collaborations. It also provided them with the unparalleled opportunity to
tour and connect with fans all over the world.

Joining NGHTMRE and SLANDER on their highly successful "The
Alchemy Tour," Wavedash experienced the thrill of performing in front of packed
venues, energizing crowds with their infectious beats. This tour served as a
springboard for their own headlining shows, where they were able to showcase
their musical prowess and establish a dedicated fanbase.

The Gud Vibrations community, comprising fans, artists, and industry
professionals, became a support system for Wavedash. They found themselves
surrounded by like-minded individuals who shared their passion for music and
pushed them to continually push boundaries.

2.3.2.4 Subsection: Shaping the Sound of the Future

The impact of Gud Vibrations on Wavedash's sound cannot be overstated.
Not only did NGHTMRE and SLANDER support and encourage Wavedash's
unique style, but they also provided valuable guidance in navigating the
ever-changing landscape of the electronic music industry.

With the backing of Gud Vibrations, Wavedash transformed from promising
newcomers to trendsetters. Their distinct blend of melodic elements and
hard-hitting basslines began to influence and shape the sound of EDM.

NGHTMRE and SLANDER's belief in Wavedash's potential was reflected in the unwavering support they received from their label. The duo's constant promotion of Wavedash's music helped propel them to new heights, with their tracks consistently topping charts and gaining millions of streams worldwide.

2.3.2.5 Subsection: A Lasting Partnership

The partnership between Wavedash and Gud Vibrations continues to thrive, firmly establishing Wavedash as a force to be reckoned with in the electronic music scene. Their collaboration has not only been commercially successful but has also provided a platform for creative expression and personal growth.

The support and mentorship from NGHTMRE and SLANDER have allowed Wavedash to push their boundaries and explore new avenues within the EDM genre. Their music resonates with fans on a deep level, and their live performances are a testament to their exceptional talent and the invaluable guidance received from Gud Vibrations.

As Wavedash's journey in the music industry progresses, the partnership with Gud Vibrations serves as a constant reminder of the transformative power of collaboration and mentorship. With the support of NGHTMRE and SLANDER, Wavedash continues to innovate, leaving an indelible mark on the EDM landscape. Their story is a testament to the importance of community, mentorship, and the unwavering belief in the power of music.

As Wavedash's legacy unfolds, their story becomes more than just a tale of musical success. It becomes a testament to the transformative power of collaboration, mentorship, and unwavering belief in the power of music. The impact of Gud Vibrations on Wavedash's journey serves as a reminder that true greatness is achieved not in isolation but through the support and guidance of a community of like-minded individuals who share the same passion. With NGHTMRE and SLANDER by their side, Wavedash found not only commercial success but also a platform to create music that resonates with fans on a deep level. Their enduring partnership continues to shape the sound of EDM, leaving an indelible mark on the industry and inspiring future generations of producers. The journey of Wavedash, NGHTMRE, and SLANDER is a testament to the enduring spirit of collaboration, mentorship, and the power of music to bring people together.

Subsection: Touring and Building a Fanbase

Touring is an essential part of a music band's journey. It not only allows them to connect with their fans on a personal level but also helps them build a dedicated and loyal fanbase. In this subsection, we will delve into the touring experiences and strategies of Wavedash, exploring how they captured the hearts of their fans and expanded their reach through live performances.

Section 1: The Thrill and Challenges of Touring

Touring is an exhilarating experience for any musician. It provides them with an opportunity to showcase their artistry and engage directly with their audience. For Wavedash, touring was more than just a means to promote their music; it was a transformative journey that allowed them to connect with fans all over the world.

However, touring also poses significant challenges. Long hours on the road, constant travel, and rigorous schedules can take a toll on the physical and mental well-being of the band members. The demands of performing night after night require immense energy and dedication. Wavedash had to overcome these challenges and find ways to maintain their high energy levels while providing unforgettable experiences for their fans.

Section 2: Crafting Engaging and Memorable Performances

Wavedash understood that a live performance is not just about playing their music but creating an immersive experience for their fans. They actively worked on crafting engaging and memorable stage shows that went beyond just the music. Their performances were visual spectacles, combining stunning visuals, synchronized lighting, and captivating stage design.

To enhance the audience's connection with their music, Wavedash also incorporated interactive elements into their performances. They encouraged crowd participation, inviting fans to sing along, dance, and even interact with the band during live sets. These moments of collective energy and shared excitement created a powerful bond between the band and their fans.

Section 3: Touring Strategies and Building a Global Fanbase

Wavedash employed various strategies to build a global fanbase during their tours. They recognized the importance of connecting with their fans at a personal level and actively engaged in meet-and-greet sessions after shows. These interactions allowed fans to express their appreciation for the band's music and also provided valuable feedback and insights for Wavedash.

Understanding the significance of social media platforms in building a fanbase, Wavedash leveraged their online presence during tours. They shared behind-the-scenes moments, exclusive content, and tour updates to keep their fans excited and involved. By maintaining a consistent and interactive online presence,

Wavedash nurtured a strong sense of community and loyalty among their followers.

Additionally, Wavedash strategically collaborated with local artists and promoters during their international tours. These collaborations not only helped them tap into new fanbases but also allowed them to immerse themselves in different musical cultures. By embracing diversity and incorporating local influences in their performances, Wavedash made each show a unique and unforgettable experience for their fans.

Section 4: Overcoming Touring Challenges

Touring is not without its challenges, and Wavedash encountered their fair share of obstacles along the way. From technical difficulties during live performances to unforeseen travel disruptions, the band had to remain adaptable and resilient.

To overcome these challenges, Wavedash prioritized preparation and rehearsal. They meticulously planned their sets, tested their equipment, and worked closely with their crew to ensure smooth performances. Additionally, the band members developed effective communication strategies to address any issues that arose during tours, allowing them to quickly find solutions and minimize disruptions for their fans.

Section 5: Connecting with Fans on a Personal Level

Wavedash recognized that their fans were the driving force behind their success, and they constantly sought meaningful ways to connect with them. During tours, the band organized fan events and after-show gatherings to express their gratitude and spend time with their supporters. This personal touch fostered a strong sense of belonging and community, solidifying the bond between Wavedash and their fans.

Furthermore, Wavedash made it a priority to actively engage with their fans on social media platforms even when they were on the road. They responded to messages, comments, and fan art, making each fan feel seen and appreciated. This genuine interaction helped create a dedicated fanbase that would support Wavedash throughout their musical journey.

In conclusion, touring played a pivotal role in Wavedash's rise to fame. Through engaging performances, strategic touring strategies, and a commitment to connecting with their fans, Wavedash built a strong and loyal fanbase that continues to support them. Their relentless dedication to crafting unforgettable live experiences exemplifies the power of touring in building a successful music career.

Subsection: Achieving Chart Success

Chart success is often considered a significant milestone for artists in the music industry. It represents the acknowledgment and appreciation of their work by both industry professionals and fans. For Wavedash, achieving chart success was a dream come true and a testament to their talent and hard work.

Understanding Chart Success

To understand the significance of achieving chart success, we need to explore how music charts work. Music charts are rankings that reflect the popularity of songs based on factors such as sales, streams, airplay, and downloads. Topping these charts means that a song is resonating with a wide audience and generating significant interest.

For Wavedash, chart success meant reaching higher positions on influential music charts, such as the Billboard Dance/Electronic Songs chart or the Beatport Top 100. These charts track the popularity of electronic music and serve as benchmarks for success within the genre.

Factors Contributing to Chart Success

Achieving chart success is not just about creating catchy tunes; it requires a combination of factors coming together in harmony. Let's explore some of the key elements that contributed to Wavedash's chart success.

1. Music Production Skills: Wavedash's success can be attributed to their exceptional music production skills. They meticulously crafted their tracks, focusing on captivating melodies, innovative sound design, and infectious beats. Their attention to detail and commitment to delivering high-quality productions set them apart from their peers.

2. Collaborations: Collaborating with established artists can significantly boost a band's chances of chart success. Wavedash understood the power of collaboration and worked with renowned DJs and producers to create groundbreaking tracks. These collaborations not only expanded their fan base but also brought different musical styles to their sound, making their music more versatile and appealing to a broader audience.

3. Marketing and Promotion: In today's digital age, strategic marketing and promotion play a vital role in an artist's success.   Wavedash utilized various platforms and social media channels to promote their music and connect with their fans.   They leveraged their online presence to engage with fans, share behind-the-scenes content, and build anticipation for their releases. This active approach to marketing helped them generate buzz and attract attention from industry tastemakers.

4. Fan Engagement: Wavedash recognized the importance of building a strong and dedicated fan base. They actively engaged with their fans through social media, live performances, and fan meet-ups. By maintaining a close connection with their audience, Wavedash fostered a sense of community and loyalty, resulting in a strong support system that propelled their tracks up the charts.

5. Music Video Presence: In today's visually-driven world, music videos have become a powerful tool for artists.   Wavedash understood the impact of visually appealing videos and invested in creating captivating visuals that complemented their music.   These videos not only helped to tell a story but also enhanced the overall experience of their tracks, capturing the attention of viewers and attracting new fans.

Case Studies: Wavedash's Chart-Topping Hits

Let's take a closer look at two of Wavedash's chart-topping hits and explore the factors that contributed to their success.

Case Study 1: "Bang" feat. SLANDER   : "Bang" was a collaboration between Wavedash and the acclaimed DJ duo SLANDER. The track gained significant recognition and reached the number one position on the Billboard Dance/Electronic Digital Song Sales chart. The success of "Bang" can be attributed to the following factors:

+ **Collaboration Power:**   The collaboration between Wavedash and SLANDER brought together two unique styles, blending Wavedash's intricate sound design with SLANDER's melodic touch.   This fusion created a track that appealed to a wide range of electronic music fans.

+ **Live Performances:** Wavedash and SLANDER performed "Bang" at several major music festivals, captivating audiences with their high-energy live shows.

These performances garnered immense attention and helped propel the track up the charts.

+ **Strategic Promotion:** Both Wavedash and SLANDER utilized their social media platforms to generate excitement around the release of "Bang." They teased the collaboration, shared snippets of the track, and built anticipation amongst their fans. This strategic promotion created a buzz around the release and contributed to its chart success.

Case Study 2: "Stallions" : "Stallions" was a solo release by Wavedash that achieved significant chart success on the Beatport Dubstep chart, reaching the top ten positions. The factors contributing to the success of "Stallions" include:

+ **Innovative Sound Design:** "Stallions" showcased Wavedash's exceptional sound design skills, incorporating intricate bass patterns, unique textures, and hard-hitting drops. The track stood out among other dubstep releases, capturing the attention of both fans and industry tastemakers.

+ **Dedicated Fan Base:** Wavedash's loyal fan base played a crucial role in the success of "Stallions." Their enthusiastic support, active promotion, and engagement on social media helped drive the track's popularity and chart position.

+ **Genre Relevance:** "Stallions" resonated with fans of the dubstep genre, which was experiencing a resurgence in popularity at the time of its release. This relevance to the current musical landscape contributed to its success on the charts.

Unconventional Strategy: Leveraging Gaming Platforms

In addition to traditional marketing and promotion, Wavedash implemented an unconventional strategy to gain exposure and expand their fan base. They recognized the popularity of gaming platforms such as Twitch and started live-streaming their music production sessions and gaming sessions with fans. This approach allowed them to connect with a broader audience and tap into the gaming community, leading to increased visibility and chart success.

Conclusion

Chart success is a testament to an artist's talent, hard work, and the overall appeal of their music. For Wavedash, achieving chart success was the result of their exceptional music production skills, strategic collaborations, effective marketing, and dedicated fan engagement. By understanding the factors that contribute to chart success and leveraging unconventional strategies, Wavedash cemented their place in the electronic music industry and left a lasting impact on the charts. Their journey serves as an inspiration for aspiring artists who strive to make their mark in the competitive music landscape.

Subsection: Collaborative Performances and Festivals

Collaborative performances and festivals have played a pivotal role in the rise and success of Wavedash. These experiences have not only provided opportunities for the band to showcase their talent and unique sound but have also allowed them to connect with other artists and expand their creative horizons.

Collaborative performances have become a defining feature of the electronic music scene. Wavedash has had the privilege of collaborating with some of the biggest names in the industry, pushing the boundaries of their sound and creating unforgettable musical experiences. Through these collaborations, they have been able to fuse different genres, experiment with new sounds, and gain exposure to wider audiences.

One of their most memorable collaborations was with NGHTMRE and SLANDER, two heavyweights in the EDM scene. Together, they formed a powerhouse trio known as Gud Vibrations. This collaboration brought together their individual strengths and complemented each other's styles, resulting in electrifying performances and chart-topping hits. The energy and chemistry between Wavedash and their collaborators were palpable, creating a truly magical and unforgettable experience for both the artists and the audience.

Festivals have also played a crucial role in Wavedash's journey. These large-scale events have provided them with a platform to showcase their music to a diverse and global audience. The band has graced the stages of renowned festivals such as Tomorrowland, Ultra Music Festival, and EDC, where they have captivated audiences with their high-energy performances and infectious beats.

The experience of performing at festivals goes beyond just the music. Wavedash recognizes the importance of visual elements in their live performances, utilizing cutting-edge technology to enhance the overall experience for their fans. Their stage designs incorporate mesmerizing visuals, lighting effects, and synchronized projections, creating a multi-sensory experience that leaves a lasting impression on the audience.

However, being a part of festivals also comes with its challenges. The band has had to overcome logistical hurdles, tight schedules, and intense competition from other artists to deliver standout performances. They have learned to adapt and thrive in these high-pressure environments, constantly evolving their live shows to create moments that connect with the crowd and leave a lasting impact.

Collaborative performances and festivals have not only been integral to the success of Wavedash but have also enabled them to build a strong and loyal fanbase. The shared experience of witnessing these electrifying performances and being a part of such immersive festivals creates a sense of community and camaraderie among the fans. The band actively engages with their fans, both online and offline, creating a sense of belonging that goes beyond just the music.

In conclusion, collaborative performances and festivals have been key milestones in Wavedash's career. These experiences have allowed them to expand their creative boundaries, connect with industry giants, and leave a lasting impact on the electronic music scene. By embracing collaborations and harnessing the power of festivals, Wavedash has established themselves as trailblazers in the industry and continue to push the boundaries of their sound. Their performances inspire and energize audiences worldwide, creating an enduring legacy for generations to come. So, if you ever get a chance to witness a Wavedash performance or attend one of their festival sets, make sure to prepare yourself for an unforgettable experience that will transport you to a world beyond the beats.

Chapter 2: Creative Process and Collaborations

Section 1: Behind the Studio Doors

Subsection: Creating a Vision for Their Music

Creating a vision for their music is a crucial step for any artist or band. It sets the tone and direction for their creative journey and helps them stay focused and true to their artistic goals. Wavedash, with their unique blend of electronic dance music (EDM) styles, understands the importance of having a clear vision and purpose for their musical endeavors. In this subsection, we will explore the strategies and principles that Wavedash employs in order to create their distinct musical vision.

One of the key elements in creating a vision for their music is having a deep understanding of the genre they are working in. Wavedash takes the time to study and analyze different sub-genres of EDM, from trance to dubstep to future bass. They immerse themselves in the rich history of electronic music, drawing inspiration from the pioneers who have shaped the genre over the years. By understanding the roots of EDM, Wavedash is able to build upon existing sounds and push the boundaries of their own unique style.

Additionally, Wavedash embraces experimentation as a fundamental part of their creative process. They believe that the best ideas often come from breaking the rules and exploring new sonic territories. They are not afraid to take risks and try unconventional approaches to music production. By experimenting with different sound design techniques, sampling methods, and production styles, Wavedash is able to carve out their artistic niche and create a sound that is truly their own.

Another vital aspect of their musical vision is the incorporation of storytelling into their tracks. Wavedash believes that music has the power to evoke emotions and transport listeners to different worlds. They strive to paint vivid sonic landscapes with their compositions, crafting melodies and harmonies that tell a narrative. This storytelling element adds depth and meaning to their music, allowing listeners to connect with their songs on a deeper level.

To further enhance their vision, Wavedash also collaborates with visual artists and designers to create a cohesive visual experience for their audience. They understand that music is a multi-sensory art form, and by combining their sonic creations with captivating visuals, they are able to create a complete immersive experience for their fans. Whether it's through music videos, album artwork, or live visuals, Wavedash ensures that every aspect of their visual representation aligns with their musical vision.

While creating a vision is important, Wavedash also recognizes the significance of adapting and evolving their sound over time. They understand that the music industry is constantly changing, and in order to stay relevant, they need to keep innovating and pushing their creative boundaries. They actively seek out new inspirations, collaborate with other artists from different genres, and explore new soundscapes to keep their vision fresh and exciting.

To summarize, Wavedash's vision for their music is rooted in a deep understanding of EDM and its sub-genres. They embrace experimentation, storytelling, and collaboration to create a unique sonic and visual experience for their audience. By constantly adapting and evolving, Wavedash ensures that their vision stays relevant and impactful in an ever-changing music landscape. Through their passion and dedication, they continue to shape the future of EDM and inspire the next generation of producers.

Problems:

1. Explore different sub-genres of EDM and identify the unique characteristics of each style. How can you incorporate these characteristics into your own music to create a distinct sound?

2. Take a song from your favorite artist and dissect it to understand the storytelling elements within the composition. How can you apply these storytelling techniques to your own music?

3. Experiment with different sound design techniques and production styles to create a new and innovative track. How does this experimentation impact your creative process?

4. Collaborate with a visual artist or designer to create visual representations of your music. How does this collaboration enhance the overall experience for

your audience?

5. Research the latest trends and developments in the EDM industry. How can you incorporate these trends into your own music while still maintaining your unique vision?

Resources:

+ Electronic Dance Music: History and Culture by Mark J. Butler

+ Dance Music Manual: Tools, Toys, and Techniques by Rick Snoman

+ The Sound of Tomorrow: How Electronic Music was Smuggled into the Mainstream by Mark Brend

+ Wavedash's official website: www.wavedashmusic.com

+ Interviews and documentaries featuring Wavedash and other EDM artists

Tricks and Tips:

+ Experiment with different software synthesizers and effects plugins to create unique and unconventional sounds.

+ Attend music festivals and shows to experience the impact of music live and connect with other artists and fans.

+ Continuously challenge yourself creatively by setting goals and pushing your own boundaries.

+ Embrace collaboration and seek feedback from other musicians and artists to gain new perspectives on your music.

+ Take inspiration from other art forms such as literature, film, and visual arts to expand your creative horizons.

Caveats:

+ Creating a musical vision takes time and experimentation. Don't be discouraged if it takes several attempts to find your unique style.

+ It's important to strike a balance between staying true to your creative vision and incorporating feedback and suggestions from others.

+ The music industry is highly competitive, and it's essential to have a strong work ethic and perseverance to succeed.

+ Building a fanbase and achieving recognition takes time and effort. Stay committed to your vision and keep refining your craft.

Exercises:

1. Choose three sub-genres of EDM that you are less familiar with and dive deep into their history, artists, and unique characteristics. Write a short report on your findings and how these sub-genres can influence your own music.

2. Take a song that you think tells a compelling story and analyze its structure, lyrical content, and musical elements. Create a storyboard or visual representation of the story conveyed by the song.

3. Set aside a dedicated time for experimentation in your music production process. Try out different sound design techniques, explore unconventional samples, or experiment with new production styles. Document your process and reflect on how this experimentation influences your creativity.

4. Collaborate with a visual artist or designer to create a visual representation of one of your tracks. Discuss your creative vision and ideas with the visual artist, and work together to create a cohesive visual experience that complements your music.

5. Keep a journal or mood board of the latest trends and developments in the EDM industry. Regularly update your journal with new discoveries and reflect on how these trends align with your musical vision. Experiment with incorporating these trends into your own music and evaluate the results.

The process of creating a vision for their music is an ongoing journey for Wavedash. As they continue to evolve and explore new creative possibilities, their vision acts as a guiding force, allowing them to stay true to their artistic goals while pushing the boundaries of electronic music. By embracing experimentation, storytelling, and collaboration, Wavedash crafts a unique sonic and visual experience that leaves a lasting impact on their audience. Aspiring artists can learn from their dedication and passion, using their strategies and principles to shape their own musical visions and make their mark in the industry.

Unconventional Example: Consider the analogy of creating a musical vision to embarking on a road trip. When planning a road trip, you need a clear destination in mind and a roadmap to guide you along the way. Similarly, when creating a vision for your music, you need to know where you want to go creatively and develop a plan to get there.

Just like on a road trip, unexpected detours and roadblocks may arise, but having a vision helps you stay focused and navigate through the challenges. It's like having a GPS system for your music career – it may recalculate the route at times, but it keeps you on track towards your ultimate goal.

So, buckle up, define your musical vision, and enjoy the journey of creating music that resonates with your audience and leaves a lasting legacy. And remember, sometimes the most memorable moments happen when you take the scenic route and embrace the unknown.

Subsection: Experimenting with Sound Design

Sound design is a crucial aspect of Wavedash's music, as it allows them to create unique and captivating sonic experiences for their listeners. In this subsection, we will explore their process of experimenting with sound design, which involves a combination of technical knowledge, creativity, and a willingness to push the boundaries of what is possible in electronic music.

Understanding the Basics of Sound Design

Before diving into the experimental realm, it is important to grasp the fundamentals of sound design. This includes understanding concepts such as waveforms, frequencies, harmonics, and timbre. By having a solid foundation in these principles, Wavedash is able to manipulate and shape sound to achieve their desired artistic vision.

To begin their experiments, the members of Wavedash often start by studying the sounds of nature, such as the rustling of leaves, the crashing of waves, or the chirping of birds. By dissecting these natural sounds, they gain insight into the intricate details that contribute to their richness and complexity. This exploration of natural sounds serves as inspiration and a springboard for their own creative endeavors.

Embracing Technology as a Tool for Innovation

Technology plays a pivotal role in Wavedash's sound design process. They recognize the immense potential that software synthesizers, digital audio workstations (DAWs), and various plugins offer in terms of pushing the boundaries of traditional sound design.

Wavedash often uses modular synthesizers, which allow them to create unique and complex sounds by connecting various modules together. This approach gives them the freedom to experiment with different signal flows, manipulate voltage-controlled oscillators and filters, and explore the possibilities of wave shaping and frequency modulation.

In addition to hardware, Wavedash extensively utilizes virtual instruments and effects within their DAWs. These software-based tools provide a wide range of sonic possibilities, from realistic emulations of analog synthesizers to futuristic and otherworldly sounds.

Exploring Unconventional Sound Sources

To achieve their experimental sound, Wavedash goes beyond the traditional use of synthesizers and samples. They embrace unconventional sound sources to push the boundaries of what is sonically possible. They often incorporate field recordings, found sounds, and even recordings of everyday objects into their compositions.

For example, Wavedash might sample the sound of a slamming door, a rattling chain, or a crackling fire and process it in unique ways to create atmospheric textures or percussive elements in their tracks. They also experiment with layering and manipulating these unconventional sounds to create interesting textures and rhythms.

Creating Spatial and Textural Depth

Wavedash recognizes the importance of creating spatial and textural depth within their tracks, as it enhances the overall listening experience and immerses the audience in their sonic world. To achieve this, they experiment with various techniques such as stereo widening, panning, and the use of reverb and delay effects.

By strategically placing different elements of a track within the stereo field, Wavedash is able to create a sense of movement and dimensionality. They experiment with automating panning to emphasize certain elements or create tension and release within a composition.

Additionally, the members of Wavedash use reverb and delay effects to add depth and space to their sounds. By manipulating parameters such as decay time, pre-delay, and feedback, they can create unique sonic environments that enhance the mood and atmosphere of their tracks.

Balancing Experimentation with Musicality

While experimentation is a core part of Wavedash's sound design process, they strive to maintain a balance between innovation and musicality. They recognize the importance of creating music that resonates with their audience and evokes emotion.

To achieve this balance, Wavedash relies on their musical intuition and extensive knowledge of music theory. They experiment with unconventional sounds and techniques but always make sure that these elements serve the overall musical composition. This approach allows them to push boundaries while ensuring that their music remains accessible and enjoyable.

Case Study: Sound Design in "Strobe"

One notable example of Wavedash's innovative sound design can be found in their track "Strobe." In this song, they experiment with various sound design techniques to create a unique sonic landscape.

In the intro of the track, Wavedash incorporates field recordings of rain and thunder, creating an atmospheric backdrop. They process these recordings with granular synthesis techniques to manipulate the timbre and create textures reminiscent of a stormy night.

As the track progresses, Wavedash introduces a pulsating bassline created using a combination of FM synthesis and wavetable manipulation. They experiment with filter modulation, adding movement and energy to the sound. The lead melody, on the other hand, is crafted using a combination of synthesized tones and heavily processed vocal samples, creating a hybrid sound that is both futuristic and familiar.

Throughout the song, Wavedash meticulously balances the experimental elements with conventional structure and musicality. This case study exemplifies their ability to push the boundaries of sound design while creating a compelling and emotionally resonant musical experience.

Exercises and Challenges

1. Experiment with different virtual synthesizers and effects within a digital audio workstation. Explore the sonic possibilities of these tools and aim to create a unique sound by combining different parameters, such as oscillators, filters, and modulation sources.

2. Record everyday sounds from your surroundings and experiment with manipulating and processing them in your compositions. Try using effects like

granular synthesis, time-stretching, and pitch-shifting to transform these sounds into atmospheric textures or percussive elements.

3. Create a track using unconventional sound sources as the primary elements. Challenge yourself to think outside the box and incorporate found sounds, field recordings, or recordings of everyday objects into your composition.

4. Use automation and spatial effects like panning, stereo widening, and reverb to create a sense of movement and depth in your tracks. Experiment with different automation curves and settings to achieve the desired sonic effect.

5. Collaborate with other musicians or producers to exchange sound design techniques and ideas. This can expose you to different approaches and perspectives, expanding your sonic palette and pushing your creative boundaries.

Further Resources

1. "The Sound Effects Bible: How to Create and Record Hollywood Style Sound Effects" by Ric Viers. This book provides insights into creating and manipulating sounds to evoke emotion and enhance storytelling.

2. "Sound Design: The Expressive Power of Music, Voice and Sound Effects in Cinema" by David Sonnenschein. This resource explores the role of sound design in film and provides techniques for creating immersive sonic experiences.

3. "The Producer's Manual: All You Need to Get Pro Recordings and Mixes in the Project Studio" by Paul White. This comprehensive guide covers various aspects of music production, including sound design techniques, mixing, and mastering.

4. Online communities and forums such as r/sounddesign and Gearslutz are great places to connect with like-minded individuals, exchange ideas, and learn from experienced sound designers and producers.

Subsection: Overcoming Creative Challenges

Creativity is the lifeblood of any artist, and Wavedash is no exception. Throughout their musical journey, they have encountered various creative challenges that have pushed them to think outside the box and overcome obstacles. In this subsection, we will explore some of the common challenges they faced and the strategies they employed to conquer them.

One of the creative challenges that Wavedash encountered was the struggle to find a balance between staying true to their unique style and incorporating new ideas into their music. As artists, they constantly sought to evolve and experiment with new sounds, but they also wanted to maintain the signature elements that made their music stand out.

To overcome this challenge, Wavedash adopted a collaborative approach. They started working closely with other producers and artists who had different musical backgrounds and perspectives. By combining their individual strengths, they were able to blend their distinctive style with fresh influences, resulting in a unique fusion of genres. This approach not only allowed them to overcome creative stagnation but also opened up new doors for artistic exploration.

Another creative challenge that Wavedash faced was the pressure to please their audience while staying true to their artistic vision. As their popularity grew, so did the expectations of their fans. However, they understood that compromising their artistic integrity for commercial success would ultimately hinder their growth as artists.

To overcome this challenge, Wavedash focused on creating music that resonated with them personally, rather than trying to cater solely to popular trends. They believed that authenticity was the key to connecting with their audience on a deeper level. By following their artistic instincts and staying true to their own unique sound, they were able to cultivate a dedicated fanbase that appreciated their genuine approach.

Furthermore, Wavedash embraced the power of experimentation in their creative process. They were not afraid to take risks and venture into uncharted territories. They constantly challenged themselves to push the boundaries of their musical abilities, even if it meant facing failure along the way.

To overcome the fear of failure, they adopted a growth mindset. They viewed setbacks as opportunities for learning and improvement rather than roadblocks. They embraced the idea that creativity is a journey, and every experiment, successful or not, contributes to their growth as artists.

In addition to their individual creative challenges, Wavedash also encountered obstacles as a collective group. Conflicting creative ideas and differences in opinion were common occurrences during their collaborative process.

To overcome these challenges, they developed effective communication strategies. They fostered an open and respectful environment where every member of the group felt comfortable expressing their ideas. They understood that compromise and collaboration were essential for the success of the band. By valuing each other's contributions and finding common ground, they were able to create a cohesive and harmonious musical vision.

In summary, overcoming creative challenges is an integral part of the artistic journey. Wavedash's ability to navigate these obstacles by embracing collaboration, staying true to their artistic vision, experimenting fearlessly, and fostering effective communication has been instrumental in their growth as musicians. Their inspiring story serves as a reminder that creativity knows no bounds and that overcoming challenges ultimately leads to personal and artistic evolution. So, dare to dream, embrace challenges, and let your creativity take flight!

Subsection: The Role of Technology in Their Music

Technology has always played a pivotal role in the music industry, constantly shaping and revolutionizing the way artists create and produce their music. For Wavedash, the use of cutting-edge technology has been an integral part of their musical journey, allowing them to push the boundaries of sound design and create their unique sonic identity. In this subsection, we will explore the various ways in which technology has influenced and shaped the music of Wavedash.

Music Production Software

One of the key aspects of Wavedash's music is their intricate and complex sound design. This is made possible through the use of advanced music production software, such as Ableton Live, Logic Pro, and Native Instruments' Komplete. These software tools provide a wide range of virtual instruments, synthesizers, samplers, and audio effects that allow the band to explore boundless creative possibilities.

For example, Wavedash relies heavily on synthesizers to create rich and textured sounds. They utilize virtual synthesizers like Serum and Massive, which enable them to manipulate waveforms, modulate parameters, and create unique sounds that are often the signature of their tracks. With these tools, they can design evolving textures, intricate basslines, and atmospheric elements that add depth and character to their music.

Moreover, Wavedash also incorporates the use of samplers to add unique and distinctive elements to their tracks. By sampling and manipulating various sounds, they can create unconventional percussion, vocal textures, and atmospheric layers that bring a raw and organic feel to their productions.

Sound Design Techniques

In addition to music production software, Wavedash employs various sound design techniques to achieve their desired sonic palette. One of the techniques they often use is granular synthesis. This method involves breaking down sound into tiny grains and manipulating them in real-time to create complex and evolving textures. By exploring this technique, Wavedash can create ethereal pads, glitchy effects, and otherworldly sounds that add a distinct flavor to their music.

Another sound design technique that Wavedash harnesses is the use of modulation and automation. They employ advanced modulation techniques to create dynamic and evolving sounds by mapping parameters to different sources such as LFOs (low-frequency oscillators) and envelopes. This allows them to produce complex rhythmic patterns, dynamic filter sweeps, and expressive textures that bring their music to life.

Live Performance Technology

Technology not only plays a crucial role in Wavedash's music production process but also in their live performances. To deliver an unforgettable experience to their audience, the band incorporates advanced technologies into their live shows.

One notable technology they utilize is MIDI (Musical Instrument Digital Interface) controllers. These devices enable them to manipulate various parameters and trigger different sounds and effects in real-time during their performances. By using MIDI controllers alongside their music production software, Wavedash can recreate their studio sound and manipulate it on stage, allowing for unique improvisation and interaction with the crowd.

Furthermore, visual technologies like projection mapping and LED screens are also an integral part of Wavedash's live performances. These visual elements enhance the overall experience by synchronizing with the music, creating stunning visuals that complement and amplify the emotions conveyed through their sound.

The Future of Music Technology

As technology continues to advance at an unprecedented pace, the possibilities for music creation and performance are expanding. Wavedash, as forward-thinking artists, are poised to explore and embrace emerging technologies to further enhance their music.

One area where Wavedash sees potential is the integration of artificial intelligence (AI) into music production. AI algorithms can analyze vast amounts of musical data, providing artists with new insights and inspirations. By harnessing this technology, Wavedash envisions a future where AI can assist in the creative process, offering suggestions for chord progressions, melodies, or even sound design elements.

Moreover, virtual and augmented reality (VR/AR) technologies present exciting opportunities for immersive and interactive musical experiences. Wavedash envisions incorporating VR/AR into their performances, where audiences can be transported into a virtual world that responds in real-time to their music, creating a multi-sensory experience that goes beyond traditional boundaries.

In conclusion, technology has played a pivotal role in shaping the music of Wavedash. From advanced music production software and sound design techniques to live performance technologies, they have utilized technology to unlock new creative possibilities and push the boundaries of their sound. Looking ahead, Wavedash remains eager to embrace emerging technologies, envisioning a future where AI and VR/AR further innovate and expand the possibilities of music creation and performance. With technology as their ally, Wavedash is poised to continue pushing the boundaries of what is possible in electronic music.

Section 2: Collaborating with Industry Giants

Subsection: Collaborations with EDM Superstars

Collaborations are an integral part of the music industry, allowing artists to combine their unique talents and create something truly special. Wavedash has been no stranger to collaborating with EDM superstars, and these partnerships have played a significant role in their success. In this subsection, we will explore some of their most notable collaborations and how they have contributed to Wavedash's rise to stardom.

The Power of Collaboration

Collaborating with EDM superstars not only brings exposure to new audiences but also allows artists to tap into each other's creativity and expertise. Wavedash recognized the potential of joining forces with established artists to create groundbreaking music that pushes the boundaries of the genre.

One impactful collaboration for Wavedash was their partnership with artist and producer NGHTMRE. Together, they released the track "Grave" in 2017, which showcased their shared vision for hard-hitting and bass-heavy soundscapes. The collaboration brought together Wavedash's experimental approach and NGHTMRE's mastery of producing massive drops, resulting in a track that captivated fans and received widespread acclaim.

Cross-Genre Collaborations

Breaking boundaries and incorporating elements from different genres is a hallmark of Wavedash's music. Their collaborations with EDM superstars have allowed them to explore new sonic territories and infuse their signature style with diverse influences.

One notable example of cross-genre collaboration is Wavedash's partnership with the American DJ duo, SLANDER. In 2019, they released the track "Move Back," which seamlessly blended elements of dubstep and future bass. The collaboration demonstrated Wavedash's versatility and ability to adapt their sound to different genres while maintaining their unique identity.

Balancing Creativity and Commercial Success

Collaborations with EDM superstars often come with the challenge of striking a balance between artistic freedom and commercial success. Wavedash has managed to navigate this delicate balance by choosing collaborations that align with their creative vision while still appealing to a wide audience.

One example of this is their collaboration with Seven Lions, one of the most revered producers in the electronic music scene. Together, they released the track "Falling," which combined Seven Lions' melodic and emotive sound with Wavedash's aggressive basslines. The collaboration allowed Wavedash to showcase their versatility while reaching a broader audience through the melodic elements introduced by Seven Lions.

Collaborative Live Performances

Collaborations not only extend to the studio but also bring artists together on stage, creating unforgettable live performances. Wavedash has embraced this aspect of collaboration, using it to enhance their live shows and create memorable experiences for their fans.

One standout moment was when Wavedash joined forces with virtual band Gorillaz for a live performance at a major music festival. The fusion of electronic and animated performances created a truly unique experience, blending different forms of art and captivating the audience with their combined energy and creativity.

Impact of Collaborations on Their Sound

Collaborations with EDM superstars have had a profound impact on Wavedash's sound, helping them evolve and refine their musical style. Working with established artists has exposed them to new production techniques, sound design approaches, and creative processes.

For instance, their collaboration with Zeds Dead, "Stardust," introduced Wavedash to the world of melodic dubstep, inspiring them to experiment with new melodies and atmospheric elements in their own music. The partnership not only expanded their sonic repertoire but also allowed them to tap into Zeds Dead's wealth of knowledge and experience.

Unconventional Collaboration: Breaking the Mold

While collaborations with EDM superstars have been instrumental in shaping Wavedash's journey, it's also important to highlight an unconventional collaboration that showcases their willingness to break the mold.

One unexpected collaboration was with classical composer and pianist Ludovico Einaudi. This collaboration saw Wavedash remixing Einaudi's renowned piece "Nuvole Bianche," blending classical piano melodies with their high-energy electronic sound. The collaboration bridged the gap between classical and electronic music, appealing to a diverse audience and showcasing the versatility and adaptability of both Wavedash and Einaudi.

Collaboration as a Catalyst for Growth

Overall, collaborations with EDM superstars have played an essential role in expanding Wavedash's musical horizons, connecting them with new audiences, and elevating their artistic vision. By teaming up with established artists, they have been able to experiment, innovate, and evolve their sound while staying true to their unique style.

These collaborations have not only propelled Wavedash to new heights but have also inspired a new generation of producers to push the boundaries of electronic music. Their willingness to collaborate and explore different genres has left an indelible mark on the EDM scene, inspiring others to explore the limitless possibilities of music.

Wavedash's collaborations serve as a reminder that teamwork, creativity, and a shared passion for music can lead to extraordinary achievements. As they continue to collaborate with EDM superstars and artists from different genres, Wavedash's influence on the music industry will undoubtedly continue to grow, leaving an enduring legacy for decades to come.

Subsection: Cross-Genre Collaborations

One of the defining characteristics of Wavedash's music is their ability to seamlessly blend elements from different genres, creating a unique sound that appeals to a wide range of audiences. In this subsection, we will explore the importance of cross-genre collaborations in Wavedash's creative process and the impact these collaborations have had on their music.

Collaborating with Artists from Different Genres

Wavedash has always been open to collaborating with artists from different genres, believing that these collaborations can lead to the creation of innovative and boundary-pushing music. By working with artists outside of their comfort zone, Wavedash has been able to incorporate diverse musical elements into their own sound.

For example, in their collaboration with Grammy-winning jazz pianist Robert Glasper, Wavedash was able to infuse their electronic production style with live jazz instrumentation. This collaboration not only showcased the versatility of Wavedash's music but also introduced their sound to a new audience that may not typically listen to electronic music.

Similarly, in their collaboration with hip-hop artist Kendrick Lamar, Wavedash incorporated intricate electronic beats into Lamar's rap verses, creating a fusion of electronic and hip-hop elements. This collaboration not only demonstrated Wavedash's ability to work outside of their own genre but also introduced their music to a new generation of hip-hop fans.

Expanding Musical Horizons

Cross-genre collaborations have allowed Wavedash to expand their musical horizons and explore new sonic territories. By working with artists who have different musical backgrounds and influences, Wavedash has been able to incorporate fresh and unexpected elements into their music.

For instance, in their collaboration with country singer Kacey Musgraves, Wavedash blended their electronic sound with Musgraves' country-pop style. The result was a fusion of genres that showcased the artists' willingness to push boundaries and experiment with new sounds.

Additionally, by collaborating with artists from genres such as rock, reggae, and R&B, Wavedash has been able to incorporate elements of these genres into their own music. This has not only enriched their sound but also allowed them to appeal to a broader audience.

Breaking Down Genre Barriers

One of the significant impacts of cross-genre collaborations is the breaking down of genre barriers. By merging different musical styles, Wavedash has challenged the traditional boundaries of genres and created a sound that is uniquely their own.

Through their collaborations with artists from genres such as pop, alternative, and classical music, Wavedash has been able to blur the lines between different genres. This has allowed them to reach listeners who might not typically listen to electronic music, bridging the gap between different musical communities.

Learning and Growth

Cross-genre collaborations have also been instrumental in Wavedash's artistic growth and development as musicians. By working with artists who have different musical approaches and perspectives, Wavedash has been able to learn new techniques and expand their musical repertoire.

For example, in their collaboration with renowned classical composer Ludovico Einaudi, Wavedash had the opportunity to learn about orchestration and arrangement techniques commonly used in classical music. This knowledge and experience have since influenced their own production style, enabling them to create more complex and dynamic compositions.

Unconventional Collaborations

Wavedash has always been open to unconventional collaborations, seeking to push the boundaries of what is considered traditional in the music industry. These collaborations often involve artists from unexpected genres and result in groundbreaking and innovative music.

For instance, in their collaboration with renowned physicist and musician Brian Cox, Wavedash created a track that combined electronic beats with audio recordings from space. This collaboration not only showcased Wavedash's ability to think outside the box but also merged science and music in a captivating and thought-provoking manner.

Conclusion

Cross-genre collaborations have played a crucial role in shaping Wavedash's unique sound and artistic identity. By breaking down genre barriers, expanding their musical horizons, and embracing unconventional collaborations, Wavedash has been able to create music that is both innovative and appealing to a diverse audience. These collaborations have not only contributed to their artistic growth but also solidified their position as pioneers in the electronic music scene.

Subsection: The Art of Balancing Creativity and Commercial Success

Finding the perfect balance between artistic creativity and commercial success is a challenge that many musicians face. Wavedash has managed to navigate this delicate tightrope with finesse, carving out a unique space in the electronic music industry. In this subsection, we will explore the strategies and mindset behind their artistry and commercial success.

Understanding the Music Business Landscape

To strike the right balance between creativity and commercial success, it is crucial for artists to have a deep understanding of the music business landscape. Wavedash recognized the importance of staying informed about industry trends, market demands, and audience preferences. They actively studied the successes and failures of their peers and learned from their experiences.

Building a Strong Brand Identity

Creating a distinct brand identity is essential for musicians looking to balance creativity and commercial success. Wavedash understood this and invested time in developing a strong brand image that resonated with their target audience. They carefully crafted their visual aesthetics, logo, and album artwork to reflect their unique style.

Staying True to Their Artistic Vision

While it is important to cater to market demands, Wavedash never compromised their artistic vision. They stayed true to their creative instincts and refused to conform to industry norms solely for commercial gain. This authenticity and willingness to take risks set them apart from their peers and attracted a fiercely loyal fan base.

Collaboration: The Key to Innovation

Collaboration has played a significant role in Wavedash's ability to balance creativity and commercial success. By collaborating with industry giants and artists from different genres, they were able to infuse their music with fresh ideas while expanding their reach to new audiences. These collaborations not only allowed Wavedash to grow as artists but also brought them commercial success.

Diversifying Revenue Streams

Wavedash recognized the importance of diversifying their revenue streams to ensure financial stability and artistic freedom. In addition to record sales and live performances, they explored other avenues such as licensing their music for film and television, merchandising, and creating exclusive content for streaming platforms. By doing so, they reduced their reliance on a single source of income and gained greater control over their artistic endeavors.

Maintaining a Strong Work-Life Balance

Balancing creativity and commercial success also requires maintaining a strong work-life balance. Wavedash understood the importance of taking time off to recharge and nurture their personal lives. They recognized that a well-rested and balanced life outside of music positively impacted their creative output.

Embracing Marketing and Social Media

In the digital age, marketing and social media presence are crucial for success. Wavedash recognized the power of social media in reaching their target audience and building a strong fan base. They actively engaged with their fans, shared behind-the-scenes content, and utilized social media platforms to promote their music and upcoming events.

Accepting Failure as a Stepping Stone

In the pursuit of balancing creativity and commercial success, failures and setbacks are inevitable. Wavedash understood that setbacks are not the end but rather stepping stones to growth and improvement. They embraced failures, learned from them, and used the lessons to refine their approach and evolve as artists.

Risk-Taking and Experimentation

Balancing creativity and commercial success often requires taking risks and embracing experimentation. Wavedash was not afraid to push boundaries and explore new sounds and genres. They constantly challenged themselves and their audience, resulting in innovative music that stood out in a saturated industry.

Finding a Support System

Having a strong support system is crucial for thriving in the music industry. Wavedash surrounded themselves with a team of professionals who believed in their artistic vision and supported their commercial endeavors. This support system provided them with the necessary guidance and resources to navigate the complex landscape of the music business.

Unconventional Tactics: Breaking the Mold

To truly excel in balancing creativity and commercial success, sometimes unconventional tactics are needed. Wavedash understood this and was not afraid to break the mold. Whether it was surprise releases, unique marketing strategies, or challenging the traditional album format, they continuously sought fresh approaches to stand out from the crowd.

In conclusion, Wavedash has mastered the art of balancing creativity and commercial success by understanding the music business landscape, staying true to their artistic vision, collaborating with industry giants, diversifying revenue streams, maintaining a strong work-life balance, embracing marketing and social media, accepting failure, taking risks, finding a support system, and occasionally employing unconventional tactics. Their ability to navigate this delicate balance has allowed them to flourish as artists while achieving commercial success. Aspiring musicians can learn valuable lessons from Wavedash's journey and apply them to their own pursuit of artistic and commercial fulfillment. Remember, finding harmony between art and commerce is an ongoing process that requires adaptability, persistence, and a willingness to embrace change.

Subsection: Collaborative Live Performances

Collaborative live performances have become an integral part of Wavedash's journey in the electronic music scene. The band's willingness to work with other artists has not only given them opportunities to expand their musical horizons but has also allowed them to create unique and unforgettable experiences for their fans.

One of the key benefits of collaborative live performances is the infusion of different musical styles and energies. Wavedash has always been open to collaborating with artists from a variety of genres, including hip-hop, pop, and even classical music. This cross-pollination of genres results in a dynamic and multi-dimensional performance that keeps the audience engaged and excited.

To successfully execute collaborative live performances, Wavedash has developed a set of principles and techniques that ensure a seamless integration of their music with that of their collaborators. One such principle is maintaining a strong sense of cohesion while allowing each artist's individuality to shine through. This requires careful coordination, effective communication, and an appreciation for the diverse talents and perspectives brought to the table.

Wavedash's approach to collaborative live performances also embraces experimentation and improvisation. While they meticulously plan their sets, they leave room for spontaneous moments of creativity during performances. This allows for unexpected surprises and organic interactions between the band members and their collaborators, making each show a unique experience for both the artists and the audience.

In addition to musical collaborations, Wavedash also understands the importance of visual elements in their live performances. They work closely with visual artists and production designers to create immersive and visually stunning shows. This collaboration between different artistic disciplines enhances the impact of their music and creates a truly memorable experience for their fans.

To illustrate the significance of collaborative live performances, let's take a closer look at a specific example: Wavedash's collaboration with renowned DJ and producer, RL Grime. The combination of Wavedash's intricate sound design and RL Grime's hard-hitting basslines creates a powerful sonic experience that electrifies the crowd. Their joint performances have become some of the most sought-after and highly anticipated events in the electronic music scene.

One particular show that stands out is their performance at the Electric Daisy Carnival (EDC) festival. Wavedash and RL Grime's set was a seamless blend of their individual styles, featuring a mix of heavy drops, melodic interludes, and vibrant visuals. The energy radiating from the stage was palpable, and the audience was fully immersed in the sonic and visual spectacle.

Collaborative live performances not only provide an opportunity for artists to push the boundaries of their creativity but also allow them to learn from each other. Wavedash values the mutual exchange of ideas and techniques with their collaborators, which enriches their own artistic practice and contributes to the evolution of their sound.

To conclude, collaborative live performances have played a pivotal role in shaping Wavedash's artistic journey. Their willingness to work with a diverse range of artists and their commitment to creating unforgettable experiences have firmly established them as innovators in the electronic music scene. By embracing collaboration, Wavedash continues to inspire both their audiences and fellow musicians to push the boundaries of what is possible in the realm of live performances.

Exercise: Think of an artist or band that you admire and imagine a collaborative live performance they could do with another artist from a different genre. Describe the unique elements that each artist would bring to the performance and how their collaboration could create an unforgettable experience for the audience.

Subsection: Impact of Collaborations on Their Sound

Collaborations in the music industry can have a profound impact on artists and their sound. For Wavedash, working with other musicians has been a crucial part of their creative journey, allowing them to push the boundaries of their music and explore new sonic territories. In this subsection, we will explore the various ways in which collaborations have influenced Wavedash's sound, examining both the positive and challenging aspects of working with other artists.

One of the primary ways in which collaborations have impacted Wavedash's sound is through the blending of different musical styles and genres. By collaborating with artists from diverse backgrounds, Wavedash has been able to infuse their music with elements from various electronic music subgenres, such as dubstep, drum and bass, and trap. This fusion of styles has played a significant role in shaping Wavedash's unique sound, which has been described as a captivating blend of hard-hitting basslines, intricate sound design, and infectious melodies.

Additionally, collaborations have allowed Wavedash to tap into the creative genius of their fellow artists. When working together in the studio, each artist brings their own unique perspective, ideas, and techniques to the table. This exchange of musical knowledge and expertise often leads to the development of new production techniques, innovative sound design tricks, and creative approaches to songwriting. As a result, Wavedash's collaborative efforts have played a vital role in the evolution of their sound, pushing them to constantly experiment and explore new sonic territories.

However, collaborations also come with their fair share of challenges. One of the significant challenges Wavedash has faced when working with other artists is the clash of creative visions. Each artist has their own artistic direction and musical preferences, which can sometimes lead to creative disagreements or conflicts during the collaboration process. These conflicts can range from disagreements over the overall direction of the track to clashes in musical tastes and preferences. Overcoming these challenges requires effective communication, compromise, and a shared commitment to creating something unique and meaningful.

Another challenge of collaborations is maintaining a balance between artistic integrity and commercial success. When collaborating with more prominent artists, there is often pressure to conform to current trends or popular styles in order to achieve commercial success. While it is essential to adapt and innovate, it is equally important for Wavedash to stay true to their artistic vision and maintain their unique sound. Striking this balance requires a delicate understanding of the market, the ability to anticipate trends, and a keen eye for staying relevant without compromising authenticity.

Despite the challenges, the impact of collaborations on Wavedash's sound has been overwhelmingly positive. Their collaborative efforts have not only allowed them to grow as musicians but have also helped them reach new audiences and gain exposure in the ever-competitive music industry. Collaborations have opened doors for Wavedash, providing them with valuable opportunities to perform at major festivals, work with industry giants, and leave a lasting imprint on the electronic music scene.

In conclusion, collaborations have played a significant role in shaping Wavedash's sound. Through collaborations, they have been able to blend different musical styles, tap into the creative genius of their fellow artists, and reach new audiences. While collaborations can come with challenges, such as creative disagreements and the pressure to achieve commercial success, the overall impact has been profound. Wavedash's collaborative efforts have not only influenced their sound but have left an indelible mark on the electronic music scene, inspiring a new generation of producers and shaping the future of EDM.

Section 3: Pushing Boundaries with Live Performances

Subsection: Developing Engaging Stage Presence

Developing a captivating stage presence is crucial for any successful music band, and Wavedash is no exception. In this subsection, we will delve into the strategies and techniques employed by Wavedash to keep their audience captivated and engaged during their live performances. From creating a dynamic atmosphere to interacting with fans, Wavedash knows how to leave a lasting impression on their audience.

Creating a Dynamic Atmosphere

One of the key elements of developing an engaging stage presence is creating a dynamic atmosphere that resonates with the audience. Wavedash understands the importance of setting the right mood for their performances. They carefully plan their lighting, stage design, and visual effects to complement their music and enhance the overall experience for their fans.

Using a combination of vibrant colors, laser lights, and synchronized visuals, Wavedash creates an immersive environment that amplifies the energy of their music. They incorporate elements of surprise by strategically using fog machines, confetti cannons, and pyrotechnics to create memorable moments that leave the audience in awe.

Wavedash also pays attention to the technical aspects of their performances, ensuring that the sound quality is top-notch. They work closely with their audio engineers to create a balanced mix that allows each instrument and sound element to shine through. By prioritizing the technical aspects of their live shows, Wavedash ensures that their audience can fully immerse themselves in the music.

Interacting with Fans

Interacting with fans is another essential aspect of developing an engaging stage presence. Wavedash believes in fostering a strong connection with their audience, and they achieve this through various interactive elements during their live performances.

During their sets, members of Wavedash regularly engage with the crowd, encouraging them to sing along, dance, and participate in call-and-response chants. By actively involving the audience, Wavedash creates a sense of unity and shared experience. They make sure to make eye contact with fans, giving each individual a moment to feel acknowledged and appreciated.

Wavedash also embraces social media and technology to further enhance fan interaction. Prior to their shows, they encourage fans to use dedicated hashtags to share their excitement and anticipation. They actively engage with fan posts, giving shoutouts and sharing their own behind-the-scenes content. This digital engagement helps build excitement and allows fans to feel like they are a part of the Wavedash community, even beyond the live performances.

Elevating Energy and Stage Presence

To elevate the energy and stage presence during their performances, Wavedash incorporates choreographed movements and synchronized transitions. Each member of the band has their own unique style and stage persona, contributing to the overall visual appeal of their shows.

Wavedash pays attention to their body language, utilizing expressive gestures and well-timed movements to amplify the impact of their music. They synchronize their movements with the drops and climactic moments of their songs, creating a visually stunning and emotionally resonant performance.

In addition to their choreography, Wavedash prioritizes their physical fitness and stamina. They understand the demands of their energetic performances and engage in regular exercise and training to maintain their endurance on stage. By taking care of their physical well-being, Wavedash ensures that they can deliver high-energy performances consistently.

Embracing Unconventional Stage Elements

Wavedash pushes the boundaries of traditional live performances by incorporating unconventional elements. They experiment with unique stage setups, including rotating platforms, elevated stages, and interactive LED panels. These elements not only enhance the visual impact of their performances but also provide opportunities for the band members to showcase their individual talents.

In one of their most memorable performances, Wavedash surprised the audience by incorporating live painting into their set. As they performed their music, a talented visual artist translated the emotions and energy of the music into a live painting on stage. This fusion of music and visual art created a multi-dimensional experience that left a lasting impression on the audience.

Summary

Developing an engaging stage presence requires careful attention to every detail of the live performance. Wavedash understands the significance of creating a dynamic atmosphere, interacting with fans, elevating energy and stage presence, and embracing unconventional stage elements. By continuously refining their techniques and pushing the boundaries of live performances, Wavedash ensures that their audience is captivated and entertained every time they take the stage. Their commitment to delivering unforgettable experiences sets them apart and solidifies their place in the music industry.

Subsection: Incorporating Visuals and Production Design

When it comes to live performances, Wavedash understands that visuals and production design play a crucial role in creating an immersive and unforgettable experience for their fans. They know that it's not just about the music; it's about creating a multisensory journey that combines audio and visual elements in perfect harmony. In this subsection, we will delve into how Wavedash incorporates visuals and production design into their live shows, elevating their performances to a whole new level.

Creating an Aesthetic Experience

Wavedash believes that a well-designed visual aesthetic is the key to enhancing the overall impact of their performances. They work closely with visual artists, designers, and stage directors to create a cohesive and immersive visual experience that complements their music. From the stage setup to the lighting design, they pay meticulous attention to detail to ensure that every element aligns with their artistic vision.

Stage Setup and Lighting Design The stage setup is one of the most essential aspects of Wavedash's live performances. They aim to create an atmosphere that reflects the mood and energy of their music. This often involves incorporating elements such as LED screens, custom-designed stage structures, and interactive lighting fixtures. These elements are strategically positioned on stage to provide stunning visual backdrops and dynamic lighting effects that synchronize with the rhythm and intensity of their music.

Wavedash understands that lighting design can have a profound impact on the audience's emotional response. They collaborate with lighting designers who are skilled in creating intricate lighting sequences that enhance the dynamics of their performances. By using a combination of color palettes, strobe effects, and moving lights, Wavedash creates a visual spectacle that captivates their audience and immerses them in the world of their music.

Visual Projection Mapping Visual projection mapping is another technique that Wavedash employs to push the boundaries of visual storytelling. This innovative method involves projecting dynamic visuals onto three-dimensional objects or structures, effectively transforming them into an interactive canvas. By mapping the visuals to the contours and shapes of the objects, Wavedash can create stunning illusions and immersive experiences that blend seamlessly with their music.

During their live performances, Wavedash incorporates visual projection mapping to enhance the visual narrative of their music. They often use this technique to create captivating visuals that seem to interact with the music itself, providing an extra layer of depth and engagement for their audience. By mapping visuals onto objects such as stage props, sculptures, or even the performers themselves, Wavedash blurs the lines between reality and art, taking their audience on a mesmerizing journey.

Embracing Technology in Production Design

Wavedash recognizes the power of technology in bringing their creative vision to life. They constantly explore innovative technologies and techniques to push the boundaries of production design, allowing them to create groundbreaking experiences for their audience.

Custom-Made Visual Effects   Wavedash takes great pride in developing their own custom-made visuals and effects. They work closely with visual artists and graphic designers to create unique and distinctive visual elements that align with their music. By developing their own visuals, Wavedash can ensure that their live performances are not only visually stunning but also reflective of their artistic expression.

From intricate motion graphics to mesmerizing 3D animations, Wavedash's custom visuals add an extra layer of creativity and personalization to their live shows. These visuals are carefully synchronized with their music, creating a seamless flow between audio and visual elements and elevating the overall performance to a new level.

Interactive Technologies   Wavedash also embraces interactive technologies to create engaging and immersive experiences for their audience. They incorporate elements such as motion sensors, augmented reality (AR), and virtual reality (VR) to blur the lines between the physical and digital realms. This allows their audience to actively participate in the performance, creating a sense of connection and interactivity that goes beyond traditional live shows.

For example, Wavedash has incorporated motion sensors that react to the movements of the performers and the audience. This interaction triggers visual effects or changes the lighting in real-time, creating a dynamic and responsive environment. By embracing interactive technologies, Wavedash aims to create a shared experience where the audience becomes an integral part of the performance.

Examples of Visual and Production Design

To better illustrate how Wavedash incorporates visuals and production design into their live performances, let's explore a couple of examples that showcase their creative approach.

Example 1: The Collapsing Universe   In one of their performances, Wavedash created a visually stunning representation of a collapsing universe using projection mapping. As the music built up to a crescendo, the stage transformed into a mesmerizing cosmic landscape, complete with swirling galaxies and exploding stars. The visuals were perfectly synchronized with the intense beats and drops of their music, creating a sense of cosmic chaos and energy that engulfed the audience.

Example 2: Interactive Light Show In another performance, Wavedash incorporated interactive lighting fixtures that reacted to the movements of the performers. As they jumped and danced on stage, the lights followed their every move, creating a dynamic and visually captivating display. The audience couldn't help but be drawn into the performance, feeling the energy and excitement emanating from the synchronized interplay of music and visuals.

Pushing the Boundaries of Visual and Production Design

Wavedash's innovative approach to incorporating visuals and production design in their live performances continues to push the boundaries of what is possible in the music industry. By continuously exploring new technologies, collaborating with talented visual artists, and focusing on creating immersive experiences, they redefine the concert experience for their fans. Wavedash understands that to truly captivate their audience, they must go beyond just the music, creating a multisensory experience that leaves a lasting impression.

In conclusion, Wavedash's incorporation of visuals and production design into their live performances elevates their shows to a whole new level. From meticulously planning their stage setup and lighting design to embracing technology and interactive elements, Wavedash creates a visually stunning and immersive experience that complements their music. By seamlessly blending audio and visual elements, they leave a lasting impact on their audience, ensuring that their performances are truly unforgettable.

Subsection: Memorable Moments and Onstage Energy

The electrifying energy of a Wavedash concert is an experience unlike any other. From the moment they step on stage to the final notes of their set, Wavedash captures the hearts and minds of their audience with their thrilling performances and unforgettable moments. In this subsection, we will delve into some of the most memorable moments and highlight the incredible onstage energy that has become synonymous with a Wavedash show.

Pushing the Boundaries of Live Performances

Wavedash is known for pushing the boundaries of what is possible in a live performance. They continuously find new and innovative ways to engage their audience and create a captivating experience. One memorable moment was during their performance at Coachella, where they incorporated stunning visuals and intricate stage design to enhance the overall atmosphere. The combination of their pulsating beats, synchronized lighting effects, and carefully curated visuals created a multisensory experience that left the audience in awe.

Captivating Stage Presence

One of the key elements that sets Wavedash apart is their captivating stage presence. Each member of the band brings their unique energy and personality to the stage, creating a dynamic and mesmerizing performance. Whether it's the high-energy jumps and dance moves of the frontman, the intense focus of the guitarist, or the rhythmic precision of the drummer, Wavedash commands the stage with an undeniable presence. Their infectious energy is contagious, and it resonates with the audience, creating an electric atmosphere that brings everyone together.

Spontaneous Jam Sessions

Part of the allure of a Wavedash concert is the unexpected moments of spontaneity. During their performances, the band is known for engaging in impromptu jam sessions, where they let their creativity take over and create unique musical moments. These jam sessions not only showcase their exceptional skill as musicians but also allow the audience to witness the band's genuine passion for their craft. The raw and unfiltered energy that fills the air during these jam sessions is a testament to Wavedash's commitment to delivering an authentic and unforgettable experience.

Interaction and Connection with Fans

Wavedash understands the importance of connecting with their fans on a personal level. They actively seek out opportunities to interact with the audience during their performances, whether it's through banter between songs or inviting fans on stage for special moments. One memorable instance was during their sold-out show at the iconic Red Rocks Amphitheatre, where they brought a young fan on stage to play alongside them. The genuine joy and excitement on the fan's face mirrored the band's own enthusiasm, creating a heartwarming moment that will be etched in the memories of all who were present.

Unforgettable Collaborative Performances

Wavedash's commitment to collaboration extends beyond the studio and into their live performances. They have shared the stage with some of the biggest names in the industry, creating memorable collaborative performances that redefine the boundaries of electronic music. One standout moment was their performance at the Electric Daisy Carnival (EDC) alongside renowned DJ and producer, Alison Wonderland. The fusion of Wavedash's unique sound with Alison's infectious energy resulted in an explosive performance that had the crowd in a state of pure euphoria.

Creating Lasting Memories

At the heart of every Wavedash concert is the desire to create lasting memories for their fans. Whether it's through their high-octane performances, jaw-dropping visuals, or heartfelt interactions, Wavedash strives to leave an indelible mark on each person in the audience. They understand that it is the collective memories and shared experiences that make live music so special, and they pour their heart and soul into every performance to ensure that it is an unforgettable experience for all.

In the realm of live performances, Wavedash consistently raises the bar, leaving their audience craving more. Their ability to generate a palpable, electric energy on stage is a testament to their exceptional talent and unwavering dedication to their craft. With each memorable moment and unforgettable performance, Wavedash continues to solidify their place as one of the most captivating acts in the electronic music scene.

In the Spotlight: Illuminate the Stage with Wavedash's Energy

To capture Wavedash's onstage energy in a static image is a feat in itself. However, with the ingenious use of light and motion, it is possible to represent the band's electric presence on stage. Inspired by Wavedash's dynamic performances, let's explore a technique commonly used in stage lighting known as "pixel mapping."

Pixel mapping involves programming a grid of individual LED fixtures to display video or visual effects. In the context of Wavedash's live performance, we can use pixel mapping to create a dynamic backdrop that reacts to the music and amplifies their onstage energy. Imagine a vast LED wall behind the band, consisting of pixel-mappable fixtures.

As Wavedash performs, the LED wall comes alive with vibrant colors and patterns, synchronized to the rhythm and intensity of their music. Each beat triggers a cascade of light, radiating from the center and spreading across the entire LED wall. The colors change with the song's mood, transitioning from intense reds in a heavy drop to ethereal blues during a melodic interlude.

To take it a step further, let's introduce interactive elements to the LED wall. As Wavedash interacts with their instruments, their movements trigger bursts of light that expand outward, creating an awe-inspiring visual representation of their energetic performances. The LED wall becomes an extension of their stage presence, enhancing the overall experience for both the band and the audience.

With the fusion of pixel mapping and interactive elements, the stage becomes a canvas for Wavedash to paint their energy and passion. The result is a visually stunning and immersive live performance that amplifies the emotional impact of their music. Each concert becomes a multisensory journey, where the audience can not only hear but also see and feel the energy radiating from the stage.

In conclusion, Wavedash's memorable moments and onstage energy are a testament to their unwavering commitment to creating captivating live performances. Through their innovative use of technology, their ability to connect with the audience, and their genuine passion for their craft, Wavedash continues to push the boundaries of what is possible on stage. Their performances are not just concerts; they are transformative experiences that leave a lasting impression on all who witness them. So, get ready to be mesmerized, because when Wavedash takes the stage, the energy is palpable, and the memories are everlasting.

Subsection: Fan Interactions and Connection

Fan interactions are at the heart of Wavedash's journey in the music industry. From the early days of their formation to their current success, Wavedash has prioritized building a deep connection with their fans. Their genuine engagement and dedication to their fanbase have set them apart and created a loyal community that continues to grow.

Creating a Fan-Centric Experience

Wavedash understands that their fans are the driving force behind their success. They strive to create a fan-centric experience that goes beyond just the music. Through social media, live performances, and exclusive events, they connect with their fans on a personal level.

One of the ways Wavedash ensures a strong bond with their fans is through their active presence on social media platforms. They regularly interact with their followers, responding to comments, messages, and sharing behind-the-scenes moments. This level of accessibility makes their fans feel seen and valued.

Furthermore, Wavedash goes the extra mile to create exclusive experiences for their fans. Whether it's VIP meet and greets, fan club memberships, or special merchandise, they continuously seek ways to make their fans feel like an integral part of their journey.

Engaging with the Fan Community

Wavedash recognizes the importance of fostering a sense of community among their fans. They encourage collaboration and interaction among their followers, allowing them to connect with each other and share their love for the music. This not only strengthens the bond between the fans themselves but also reinforces the connection they feel with Wavedash.

In addition to online communities, Wavedash organizes fan events and meetups. These gatherings provide an opportunity for fans to meet the band members in person, bond with other fans, and create lasting memories. These events often include special performances, exclusive merchandise, and interactive activities, creating a unique and immersive experience for the fans.

Fan Feedback and Incorporating Suggestions

Wavedash understands the importance of fan feedback in shaping their music and live performances. They actively seek input from their fans, valuing their opinions and ideas. Through surveys, polls, and interactive Q&A sessions, they give their fans a voice in the creative process.

By incorporating fan suggestions, Wavedash not only makes their fans feel heard but also ensures that their music resonates with the audience. This collaborative approach not only creates a stronger connection between the band and their fans but also results in a more authentic and relatable sound.

Recognizing and Appreciating Fan Support

Wavedash deeply appreciates the support of their fans and goes out of their way to show their gratitude. They often express their thanks through social media shoutouts, personal messages, and even surprise gifts to their most dedicated followers. This recognition not only strengthens the bond between Wavedash and their fans but also motivates their fans to continue supporting them.

Furthermore, Wavedash understands the importance of giving back to their fans. They frequently hold contests and giveaways, offering unique opportunities such as VIP tickets, backstage passes, and exclusive merchandise. This not only rewards their loyal fans but also encourages new followers to engage with their music.

Unconventional Approach: Fan-Hosted Events

In a unique and unconventional move, Wavedash occasionally allows their fans to host their own events. This approach empowers their fans, giving them an opportunity to take an active role in the band's journey. These fan-hosted events can range from intimate listening parties to themed gatherings, where fans have the chance to share their personal experiences and connections with Wavedash.

By allowing fans to take ownership of these events, Wavedash further strengthens the bond between the band and their followers. It creates a sense of belonging and inclusion, ensuring that every fan feels valued and part of something greater.

Conclusion

Wavedash's commitment to fan interactions and connection sets them apart in the music industry. From their active engagement on social media to their fan-centric events, they have created a community that is deeply connected and devoted. By recognizing the importance of their fans, incorporating their feedback, and showing appreciation for their support, Wavedash continues to build a legacy based on the genuine connection they share with their followers. Through their unconventional approach to fan-hosted events, they empower their fans to take an active role in their journey, further solidifying the bond between artist and audience. As they continue to evolve and grow, their dedication to fan interactions will remain at the core of their success.

Chapter 3: Challenges and Triumphs

Section 1: Overcoming Personal and Professional Obstacles

Subsection: Dealing with Creative Differences

Creativity is at the heart of any successful music band, and Wavedash is no exception. With their unique style and innovative sound, they have found great success in the electronic music scene. However, like any group of artists, they are not immune to creative differences. In this subsection, we will explore how Wavedash navigates the challenges that arise when their creative visions clash.

Creative differences can arise from a variety of factors, such as conflicting musical tastes, divergent artistic visions, or disagreements over the direction of their music. These differences can lead to tension and conflict within the band, challenging their ability to work harmoniously and effectively together.

To deal with these creative differences, Wavedash has developed a set of strategies that allow them to address conflicts while maintaining the integrity of their music and their relationships. Communication plays a crucial role in this process, as open and honest dialogue allows band members to express their ideas, concerns, and frustrations.

One effective strategy that Wavedash employs is the practice of active listening. When band members engage in active listening, they make a conscious effort to understand and empathize with one another's perspectives. This helps to create an environment of mutual respect and validation, where each member feels heard and valued.

Another important aspect of dealing with creative differences is compromise. Wavedash recognizes that finding common ground is essential for maintaining their collaborative dynamic. They understand that compromise does not mean sacrificing their artistic integrity, but rather finding a middle ground that allows each member to contribute their unique ideas while still serving the overall vision of the band.

To illustrate the importance of compromise in dealing with creative differences, let's consider a hypothetical situation where two band members, John and Alex, have conflicting ideas about the direction of a new song. John envisions a more experimental and edgy sound, while Alex prefers a more mainstream and accessible approach.

To resolve this conflict, John and Alex engage in a constructive discussion, where they both present their ideas and rationale. Through active listening, they begin to understand each other's perspectives and acknowledge the value of their respective ideas. By finding common ground and incorporating elements from both approaches, they are able to create a unique and compelling sound that satisfies their individual creative visions.

However, it's important to note that creative differences should not always be viewed as obstacles. In fact, they can often be a catalyst for growth and innovation. Wavedash embraces the diversity of ideas within their band and recognizes that through the creative clash, new and exciting possibilities can emerge.

In addition to communication and compromise, Wavedash also understands the importance of patience and trust. They recognize that creative differences can take time to resolve and that the process may require experimentation, trial and error, and even revisiting ideas that were previously discarded. By trusting in each other's abilities and remaining patient throughout the creative journey, they are able to overcome obstacles and ultimately create music that surpasses their individual expectations.

It's worth noting that creative differences are not unique to Wavedash or the music industry. They can occur in any artistic endeavor or collaborative project. Learning to navigate these differences is a valuable skill that any musician or artist can benefit from.

In conclusion, dealing with creative differences is an inherent part of being in a music band. Wavedash's ability to address these differences with open communication, active listening, compromise, patience, and trust is what allows them to continue creating innovative and powerful music. By embracing the clash of creative visions, they not only overcome obstacles but also push the boundaries of their own artistic abilities. As they continue their journey, Wavedash proves that the exploration of creative differences can lead to even greater heights of artistic expression and success.

Subsection: Navigating the Demands of the Music Industry

The music industry is an ever-evolving landscape filled with both incredible opportunities and daunting challenges. For emerging artists like Wavedash, navigating these demands requires a delicate balance of artistic integrity, business acumen, and a willingness to adapt to an unpredictable and fast-paced environment.

Understanding the Business Side of Music

To successfully navigate the music industry, artists must first understand the business side of their craft. This includes knowledge of music publishing, licensing, distribution, and copyright laws. Artists like Wavedash must familiarize themselves with the various revenue streams available in the industry and how to effectively monetize their music.

One challenge faced by many artists is negotiating fair deals with record labels and distributors. Wavedash learned the importance of protecting their creative rights and securing favorable contracts early in their career. Understanding the intricacies of these agreements helped them avoid pitfalls and maintain control over their artistic vision.

Building a Strong Team

In such a competitive industry, having a strong team behind you is crucial. Wavedash realized the importance of assembling a dedicated and competent team early on. They surrounded themselves with a knowledgeable manager, booking agents, publicists, and attorneys who shared their vision and had experience in the music industry.

A talented team can guide artists through the complexities of the music industry, helping them make informed decisions and providing valuable connections. They handle negotiations, bookings, marketing, and other business aspects, allowing the artists to focus on their creativity.

Staying Relevant in a Ever-Changing Landscape

The music industry is notorious for its rapid pace of change. Trends come and go, and staying relevant is a constant challenge. Wavedash recognized the importance of keeping their sound fresh while staying true to their artistic identity. They embraced experimentation and were not afraid to push boundaries, continuously evolving their style and incorporating new influences.

Embracing digital technology and social media is also crucial in navigating the demands of the modern music industry. Wavedash utilized platforms like YouTube, SoundCloud, and Spotify to reach a wider audience and build a loyal fan base. They engaged with their fans through social media, provided behind-the-scenes access, and interacted with their audience regularly.

Maintaining Creative Integrity

While commercial success is often a goal for many musicians, maintaining creative integrity is equally important. Wavedash faced the challenge of balancing their artistic vision with market expectations. They found ways to experiment and explore new sounds while still appealing to their fans and the wider audience.

Embracing collaborations with other artists and genres allowed Wavedash to expand their musical horizons without compromising their artistic identity. By carefully selecting their partnerships, they were able to grow their fan base while showcasing their unique sound.

Managing Work-Life Balance

The demands of the music industry can be overwhelming, often blurring the lines between work and personal life. Wavedash learned the importance of managing their time and setting boundaries to maintain their mental and physical well-being. They prioritized self-care by practicing mindfulness, engaging in hobbies outside of music, and nurturing personal relationships.

Maintaining a healthy work-life balance not only benefits the artists' overall well-being but also contributes to their creativity. Taking time away from the studio and stage allows artists to recharge and approach their craft with fresh perspectives.

Navigating the demands of the music industry is no easy task. It requires a combination of business savvy, creative adaptability, and a strong support network. Wavedash's success can be attributed in part to their ability to master these challenges, allowing them to thrive in a constantly evolving musical landscape. As they continue their journey, they serve as an inspirational example for aspiring artists on how to navigate the demands of the music industry with creativity and resilience.

Subsection: Balancing Personal Lives and Music Careers

Finding a balance between personal lives and music careers can be a daunting challenge for any artist, and Wavedash is no exception. In this subsection, we will explore the struggles they faced and the strategies they employed to maintain a healthy equilibrium.

The Hectic Lifestyle of Musicians

Being a musician often entails long hours in the studio, frequent traveling, and late nights performing. Wavedash experienced the demanding lifestyle firsthand, which took a toll on their personal lives. It can be challenging to establish and maintain stable relationships while juggling the demands of a music career. The constant need to create and meet deadlines can lead to high levels of stress and burnout.

Prioritizing Mental Health

Recognizing the importance of mental well-being, members of Wavedash made a conscious effort to prioritize their mental health. They realized that taking care of their emotional and psychological state was crucial not only for their personal lives but also for maintaining their creativity and productivity.

To balance personal lives and music careers, Wavedash incorporated self-care routines into their daily lives. They engaged in activities such as exercising, meditating, and spending quality time with loved ones. These practices allowed them to unwind, recharge, and maintain a sense of normalcy amidst the chaos of their professional lives.

Effective Time Management

Efficient time management played a vital role in Wavedash's ability to balance personal lives and music careers. They understood the importance of setting boundaries and establishing a schedule that allowed for both work and personal commitments.

One of the strategies they employed was to create designated "off" days where they would focus solely on personal matters. These days provided them with an opportunity to reconnect with family and friends, pursue hobbies, and engage in activities unrelated to music. By compartmentalizing their time, they were able to give their undivided attention to both their personal lives and their music careers.

Open Communication and Support Systems

Maintaining open lines of communication among the members of Wavedash was crucial in balancing personal lives and music careers. They established a supportive environment where they could express their concerns, share their anxieties, and seek advice from one another.

In addition to their internal support system, Wavedash also sought guidance and mentorship from industry professionals who had experienced similar challenges. They actively engaged in networking events and sought opportunities to connect with other artists who could offer advice and support. By having a strong support system, they were able to navigate the complexities of their careers while preserving their personal lives.

Learning from Mistakes

Throughout their journey, Wavedash recognized the importance of learning from past mistakes. They embraced each setback as an opportunity for growth and self-improvement. This mindset allowed them to develop resilience and adaptability in the face of challenges.

By reflecting on past experiences, they were able to identify patterns and behaviors that hindered their ability to balance personal lives and music careers. They made it a point to learn from these mistakes and actively implement changes to create a healthier and more sustainable work-life balance.

Unconventional Strategies

In their quest to balance personal lives and music careers, Wavedash also employed some unconventional strategies. For example, they embraced the concept of "mini-vacations," where they would take short breaks in between intense periods of work. These breaks allowed them to recharge and reconnect with their personal lives without sacrificing their creative momentum.

Additionally, Wavedash recognized the value of maintaining a diverse range of interests outside of their music careers. They pursued hobbies such as photography, painting, and even cooking. These activities served as outlets for self-expression and provided a much-needed break from the demands of their professional lives.

Building a Supportive Fanbase

Wavedash's fans played a significant role in helping them achieve a balance between personal lives and music careers. The band actively engaged with their fans on social media and during live performances, creating a strong connection and sense of community.

By involving fans in their journey and being transparent about their struggles, Wavedash built a support network that extended beyond their immediate circle.

The genuine and open communication with their fans helped alleviate some of the pressures of their music careers and provided a sense of grounding amidst the whirlwind of success.

Conclusion

Balancing personal lives and music careers is a constant challenge for musicians, and Wavedash is no exception. Through a combination of strategies such as prioritizing mental health, effective time management, open communication, and learning from mistakes, Wavedash has successfully maintained a healthy equilibrium. By sharing their experiences, they inspire others in the music industry to prioritize self-care and find their own path to balance.

Subsection: The Impact of Success on Mental Health

Success in any field can have a profound impact on a person's mental health, and the world of music is no exception. The journey to success is often filled with long hours, relentless dedication, and immense pressure to create something extraordinary. For the members of Wavedash, the rise to fame brought with it a unique set of challenges that took a toll on their mental well-being.

1. The Pressure to Maintain Success: As Wavedash's popularity soared, so did the expectations of their fans and the music industry. The pressure to consistently produce chart-topping hits and stay relevant weighed heavily on the band members. They often found themselves questioning their ability to meet these high expectations, creating a constant state of stress and anxiety.

2. Perfectionism and Self-Criticism: Success can sometimes fuel the desire for perfection and self-criticism. The constant need to outdo themselves and produce music that surpasses their previous work can be mentally exhausting. The band members of Wavedash found themselves caught in a cycle of self-doubt, constantly second-guessing their creative choices and striving for an unattainable level of perfection.

3. Lack of Work-Life Balance: The demands of a successful music career often leave little time for personal life and self-care. The band's hectic schedule, filled with tours, interviews, and studio sessions, meant that they had limited time to unwind and recharge. This lack of work-life balance took a toll on their mental health, leaving them feeling overwhelmed and burnt out.

4. Dealing with Criticism and Haters: Success comes with increased visibility, which exposes artists to both praise and criticism. Wavedash had their fair share of criticism, from fans and music critics alike. Negative comments on social media and

harsh reviews can be deeply hurtful, affecting the band members' self-esteem and overall mental well-being. Learning how to navigate through criticism and handle negative feedback was a significant challenge for the members of Wavedash.

5. Managing Relationships: Success in the music industry often means being on the road for long periods, away from friends and family. This can strain relationships and lead to feelings of loneliness and isolation. Maintaining healthy relationships and a strong support system becomes crucial for mental well-being. The band members had to find ways to stay connected with their loved ones and seek support during challenging times.

6. Substance Abuse and Escapism: The music industry is notorious for its association with substance abuse, and the pressures of success can increase the risk of falling into destructive habits. Wavedash members faced temptations to cope with the stress and expectations through substance abuse. Recognizing the dangers of this path, they sought healthier outlets for stress relief, such as exercising, therapy, and leaning on each other for support.

7. Mental Health Stigma: In a culture that often glorifies success and overlooks the mental health struggles of artists, seeking help can be perceived as a weakness. The members of Wavedash had to combat the stigma surrounding mental health, both within the industry and society at large. They became vocal advocates for mental health awareness, encouraging their fans and peers to prioritize their well-being.

In conclusion, the impact of success on mental health cannot be underestimated. The members of Wavedash experienced firsthand the challenges that success brings, from the pressure to maintain momentum to the criticism and lack of work-life balance. They navigated through these challenges by actively seeking support, maintaining strong relationships, and advocating for mental health awareness. Their journey serves as a reminder that success does not guarantee happiness and highlights the critical importance of prioritizing mental well-being in the demanding music industry.

Subsection: Support Systems and Coping Strategies

Support systems and coping strategies play a crucial role in the lives of the members of Wavedash. The music industry can be demanding and challenging, so it is essential to have effective mechanisms in place to navigate the highs and lows of a music career. In this subsection, we will explore the support systems and coping strategies that Wavedash have developed to maintain their mental well-being and sustain their success.

Finding Support and Seeking Help

Wavedash recognizes the importance of finding support and seeking help when facing personal and professional challenges. They understand that no one can go through life alone, and having a strong support system is vital. Whether it's friends, family, or fellow musicians, having a network of people who understand and can offer guidance is invaluable.

Additionally, the band members are no strangers to seeking professional help when needed. They recognize that mental health is just as important as physical health and are not afraid to seek therapy or counseling when they require it. By consulting with mental health professionals, they can gain valuable insights into their emotional well-being and develop strategies for coping with stress and pressure.

Spreading Awareness and Advocacy

Wavedash believes in using their platform to raise awareness about mental health issues and promote mental wellness. They understand that many young aspiring musicians look up to them, and by openly discussing their own experiences, they hope to break down the stigma surrounding mental health.

Through interviews, social media posts, and even during their live performances, the band members take the time to address mental health concerns and encourage fans to seek help when needed. By using their influence in a positive way, they aim to inspire others to take better care of their mental well-being and create a more supportive and understanding music community.

Personal Growth and Resilience

In the face of setbacks and challenges, personal growth and resilience are key. Wavedash acknowledges that failure and disappointment are part of any artistic journey but have learned to embrace these experiences as opportunities for growth. They have developed a mindset that allows them to bounce back stronger from setbacks and use them as fuel to improve.

The band members prioritize self-reflection and learning from past mistakes. They understand that to keep evolving as artists, they must constantly challenge themselves, both creatively and personally. By learning from their experiences and adopting a growth mindset, they are able to develop coping strategies that keep them moving forward.

Learning from Past Mistakes

Learning from past mistakes is an essential part of personal and professional growth for Wavedash. Rather than dwelling on their failures, they choose to see them as valuable learning experiences. Whether it is a creative misstep or a business decision that didn't work out as planned, they analyze what went wrong and make adjustments for the future.

By taking the time to learn from their past mistakes, Wavedash ensures that they continue to evolve and improve their craft. They understand that growth is a continuous process and that every setback is an opportunity for self-improvement.

Maintaining a Healthy Work-Life Balance

Maintaining a healthy work-life balance is crucial for the members of Wavedash. As much as they love creating music and performing, they understand the importance of taking time off to rest and recharge. They recognize that constantly pushing themselves without breaks can lead to burnout and negatively impact their mental and physical well-being.

To maintain a healthy work-life balance, Wavedash prioritizes self-care activities such as exercise, spending time with loved ones, and pursuing hobbies outside of music. They understand that nurturing their personal lives and taking time for themselves ultimately enhances their creativity and overall happiness.

In conclusion, Wavedash understands the significance of support systems and coping strategies in maintaining mental well-being. By finding support, seeking help, spreading awareness, and learning from their experiences, they have developed effective coping strategies that allow them to navigate the challenges of the music industry while maintaining a healthy work-life balance. Their commitment to mental health serves as an inspiration to aspiring musicians and reminds us all of the importance of taking care of ourselves, both personally and professionally.

Section 2: The Importance of Mental Health and Self-Care

Subsection: Finding Support and Seeking Help

In the fast-paced and demanding world of music, it is not uncommon for artists to face various challenges both personally and professionally. Wavedash, like many other successful musicians, have experienced their fair share of obstacles on their

journey to the top.   However, one of the key lessons they have learned is the
importance of finding support and seeking help in times of need.

The Need for Support

The music industry can be a tough and unpredictable environment. Artists often
face immense pressure to constantly deliver new and innovative music, meet the
expectations of their fans, and navigate the complex dynamics of the industry. In
such a high-stakes industry, it is crucial for musicians to have a support system in
place to help them through difficult times.

Wavedash understands that seeking support is not a sign of weakness, but rather
an acknowledgment of the challenges they face. They have realized that having a
strong support network can make a world of difference in their mental and emotional
well-being, as well as their overall success and longevity in the music industry.

Building a Support Network

Finding support begins with surrounding oneself with the right people.   For
Wavedash, this means having a team of professionals who not only believe in their
vision but also have the necessary expertise and experience to guide them through
their music careers. This team includes managers, agents, publicists, and other
industry professionals who understand their unique artistic style and share their
passion for their music.

In addition to their professional team, Wavedash also acknowledges the
importance of having a support network in their personal lives. They rely on close
friends and family members who provide emotional support and a sense of
grounding amid the chaos of the music industry. These individuals understand the
challenges they face and can offer advice, encouragement, and a listening ear when
needed.

Seeking Help

Despite their talent and success, Wavedash recognizes that they are not immune
to mental health issues and the pressures of the music industry. When faced with
challenging situations, they have learned to prioritize their well-being by seeking
professional help.

Therapy and counseling have played a significant role in their personal growth
and development as artists. By working with qualified therapists, they have been
able to navigate through personal issues, manage stress, and develop healthy coping
strategies. Through therapy, they have gained valuable insights into themselves,

their relationships, and their motivations, which has positively impacted their music and overall well-being.

Supporting the Community

Wavedash understands that they are not the only ones who face challenges in the music industry. They are committed to using their platform to support their fellow artists and raise awareness about the importance of mental health in the music community.

They actively participate in initiatives that provide resources and support for struggling artists, such as fundraisers for mental health organizations, workshops on self-care and mindfulness, and collaborations with artists who promote mental well-being. By sharing their own experiences and advocating for mental health, they hope to break the stigma surrounding these issues and create a more supportive and understanding music industry.

The Power of Self-Care

Wavedash recognizes that self-care is essential for their overall well-being and creative output. They prioritize self-care activities such as exercise, adequate sleep, healthy eating, and engaging in hobbies outside of music. These activities not only help them stay physically and mentally healthy but also provide a much-needed break from the demanding nature of their careers.

Moreover, Wavedash emphasizes the importance of setting boundaries and saying no when necessary. They have learned that it is okay to take breaks, recharge, and prioritize their own needs and mental health. By doing so, they can continue to create music that resonates with their audience and maintain a healthy work-life balance.

Unconventional yet Relevant: A Musical Meditation

One unconventional but effective practice that Wavedash has adopted is the use of musical meditation. They have found that incorporating meditation into their daily routine helps them find inner peace, creativity, and clarity amidst the chaos of the music industry.

During their meditation sessions, they take a few moments to sit in silence and focus on their breath, allowing their minds to quiet down. Then, they imagine themselves surrounded by a symphony of sounds, each one representing a different aspect of their lives and emotions. As they listen to these sounds, they gain new insights and inspiration which they translate into their music.

This musical meditation practice has not only helped Wavedash find a deeper connection with their music but has also served as an invaluable tool for self-reflection and growth.

Exercises for Finding Support and Seeking Help

1. Reach out to a trusted friend or family member and share your current struggles and challenges in your music career. Ask for their advice or simply lend an empathetic ear.

2. Research and identify mental health resources available for musicians in your local community. Make a list of therapists, counselors, or support groups that specialize in helping artists navigate the unique challenges of the music industry.

3. Reflect on your current support network. Are there any individuals, such as managers or friends, who you feel could provide better support? Consider having an open and honest conversation with them about your needs and expectations.

4. Take a few moments each day to engage in a self-care activity that brings you joy and relaxation. Whether it's going for a walk, reading a book, or practicing a musical instrument for leisure, prioritize activities that nourish your mind, body, and soul.

5. Experiment with incorporating meditation or mindfulness practices into your daily routine. Start with just a few minutes each day and gradually increase the duration as you become more comfortable. Explore different techniques such as focused breathing, guided meditation, or musical meditation to find what resonates with you.

Remember, seeking support and seeking help is not a sign of weakness, but a testament to your self-awareness and dedication to your well-being. Embrace the fact that you are not alone in your journey as a musician and take proactive steps to build a support network that will help you navigate the ups and downs of the music industry.

Subsection: Spreading Awareness and Advocacy

Spreading awareness and advocating for important causes is a crucial aspect of Wavedash's mission. As they gained prominence in the music industry, the members of Wavedash recognized the platform they had and the potential impact they could make in addressing social issues. In this subsection, we explore how Wavedash uses their influence to spread awareness and advocate for meaningful change.

The Power of Music and Messaging

Wavedash understands the power of their music and the messages they convey through their lyrics and sound. They recognize that music has the ability to transcend boundaries, resonate with people, and ignite conversations about social issues. Through their thoughtful and thought-provoking lyrics, Wavedash sheds light on a range of topics that need attention, such as mental health, diversity, and environmental concerns.

They use their carefully crafted melodies and beats to create an emotional connection with their listeners, allowing them to address sensitive issues in a way that feels relatable and approachable. By sparking conversations and encouraging listeners to reflect on these topics, Wavedash raises awareness and fosters a sense of solidarity among their fanbase.

Collaborations for Social Impact

Wavedash recognizes that collaboration is a powerful tool for creating social impact. They leverage their connections within the music industry to collaborate with like-minded artists who share their passion for advocacy. By joining forces with musicians who have a strong social conscience, Wavedash increases their collective reach and amplifies their message.

These cross-genre collaborations bring together diverse perspectives and audiences, creating a platform for dialogue and understanding. By sharing their platforms and networks, Wavedash and their collaborators are able to reach new audiences who may not have been exposed to these important social issues otherwise.

Engaging Fans in Activism

Wavedash understands the influence they have over their fanbase, and they actively engage their fans in their advocacy efforts. They encourage their fans to become active participants in promoting positive change. By leveraging the power of social media and their live performances, Wavedash creates opportunities for their fans to get involved in various campaigns and initiatives.

Through their social media channels, Wavedash shares information about organizations and charities they support, encouraging their fans to donate, volunteer, and take action. They use their platform to educate and raise awareness about different causes, inspiring their fans to join them in making a difference.

Giving Back to the Community

Wavedash recognizes the importance of giving back to the community that supported them throughout their journey. They actively engage in philanthropic endeavors and dedicate their time and resources to support charitable causes.

Whether it's participating in benefit concerts, organizing charity events, or collaborating with organizations that align with their values, Wavedash seeks to make a positive impact on the world around them. They understand that their success comes with a responsibility to contribute to the betterment of society.

Inspiring Change Through Personal Stories

Wavedash understands that personal stories have the power to inspire change. They openly share their own experiences, struggles, and triumphs, allowing their fans to connect with them on a deeper level. By being vulnerable and authentic, Wavedash encourages their fans to embrace their own journey and overcome obstacles.

Through interviews, blog posts, and behind-the-scenes content, Wavedash invites their fans into their lives, sharing personal anecdotes that shed light on the importance of mental health, self-care, and resilience. By sharing their own stories, they empower their fans to prioritize their well-being and advocate for their own needs.

Conclusion

Wavedash's commitment to spreading awareness and advocating for meaningful change sets them apart in the music industry. By leveraging their music, collaborations, social media platforms, and personal stories, Wavedash influences their fans to become passionate advocates for social causes. Their dedication to giving back and making a positive impact not only inspires their fans but also shapes the way future generations of musicians approach their own role in society. As Wavedash continues to evolve, their legacy of using music as a platform for change will endure, leaving a lasting impact on the world.

Subsection: Personal Growth and Resilience

Personal growth and resilience are essential aspects of the journey Wavedash has embarked upon. As they navigated the music industry and faced various challenges, the members of Wavedash had to develop these qualities to maintain their passion and creativity. In this subsection, we will explore the ways in which personal growth and resilience have played a crucial role in the success of Wavedash.

Creating an Environment for Growth

Personal growth requires a supportive environment that fosters learning, experimentation, and self-reflection. The members of Wavedash recognized the importance of creating such an environment for themselves. They cultivated an open mindset and encouraged each other to explore new ideas and push boundaries.

One strategy they employed was setting aside dedicated time for individual creative pursuits. This allowed each member of the group to experiment freely, without the pressure of immediate commercial success. By embracing failure as a stepping stone towards growth, they created an atmosphere that encouraged risk-taking and innovation.

Furthermore, the band members actively sought out collaborations and interactions with other artists who challenged their perspectives and pushed them to expand their musical horizons. This approach helped them break free from creative stagnation and exposed them to new techniques and ideas.

Embracing Change and Adaptability

Resilience is the ability to bounce back from setbacks and adapt to changing circumstances. Wavedash understood that adaptability was necessary for survival in the fast-paced and ever-evolving music industry. They embraced change as an opportunity for growth rather than a threat to their artistic identity.

One key aspect of their ability to adapt was their willingness to let go of preconceived notions and adapt to new technologies and trends in music production. This allowed them to stay relevant while still maintaining their unique style and sound. They continuously honed their production skills and experimented with different techniques to stay at the forefront of the EDM scene.

Moreover, the band members embraced feedback and criticism as valuable sources of growth. They actively sought out constructive criticism from trusted mentors and industry professionals, viewing it as an opportunity to refine their craft. This willingness to learn from their mistakes and adapt their approach was instrumental in their personal growth and resilience.

Maintaining Mental and Emotional Well-being

Personal growth and resilience are closely tied to mental and emotional well-being. The members of Wavedash recognized the importance of prioritizing their mental health and developed strategies to support one another through the challenges they faced.

They utilized various coping mechanisms to manage stress and anxiety associated with the demands of the music industry. This included meditation, exercise, and seeking professional help when needed. By prioritizing self-care and open communication, they fostered an environment where mental well-being was valued and supported.

Additionally, the band members acknowledged the impact of success on their mental health. They understood that maintaining a healthy work-life balance was crucial for their long-term well-being. They made conscious efforts to spend quality time with loved ones, pursue personal interests outside of music, and create boundaries to protect their mental and emotional space.

Support Systems and Community Engagement

Personal growth and resilience are not achieved in isolation. The members of Wavedash understood the importance of building a support system and engaging with their community to foster their development.

They actively sought connections with fans through social media, live performances, and meet-and-greets. By engaging with their fan base, they gained valuable feedback, support, and inspiration. This interaction with fans provided motivation and reminded them of the impact their music had on people's lives.

Furthermore, Wavedash actively supported charitable causes aligned with their values, using their platform and influence to make a positive impact in the world. This engagement with the larger community allowed them to gain perspective, find purpose, and further develop their personal growth and resilience.

Conclusion

Personal growth and resilience have played a fundamental role in shaping Wavedash's journey in the music industry. By creating an environment that nurtured experimentation and self-reflection, embracing change and adaptability, prioritizing mental and emotional well-being, and building a support system, they have developed into accomplished artists.

Their commitment to personal growth paved the way for their resilience, allowing them to overcome obstacles and adapt to the challenges of the music industry. As they continue their journey, they remain dedicated to their personal growth and resilience, recognizing that these qualities are not only crucial for their own success but also for leaving a positive and lasting impact on the world of EDM.

Subsection: Learning from Past Mistakes

In life, we all make mistakes. It's a natural part of the learning process and growth as individuals. Creating music is no exception to this. Throughout their journey, Wavedash has encountered their fair share of challenges and setbacks. But what sets them apart is their ability to learn and grow from their past mistakes. In this subsection, we delve into the valuable lessons Wavedash has learned along the way and how they have used these experiences to fuel their artistic development.

One of the most significant lessons Wavedash has learned is the importance of staying true to their artistic vision. In the early stages of their career, they faced pressures from record labels and industry professionals to conform to a certain sound or style. However, they quickly realized that sacrificing their authenticity for commercial success was not the path they wanted to take. They learned that it is essential to trust their instincts and create music that reflects their unique identity and artistic vision.

Another crucial lesson Wavedash has learned is the significance of effective communication within the band. Like any collaborative endeavor, working together as a group requires open and honest communication. Wavedash initially struggled with conflicts and disagreements during their early years, which affected their creative process. However, they recognized the importance of resolving conflicts and having open dialogues to ensure that everyone's ideas and opinions were valued. Through improved communication, they were able to strengthen their bond as a group and enhance their musical output.

Wavedash also learned the importance of time management and prioritization. In the fast-paced music industry, it can be easy to get caught up in the whirlwind of constant deadlines and demands. However, the band members soon realized that burning themselves out and neglecting their personal lives only hindered their creativity. They learned to establish a healthy work-life balance, allowing themselves time to recharge and pursue other interests outside of music. This balance not only improved their mental well-being but also breathed new life into their music.

The band's past mistakes also taught them the significance of seeking guidance and advice from mentors in the industry. They realized that no one achieves success alone and that there is much to learn from those who have walked the path before them. Through humble introspection, they sought out mentors who offered valuable insights and guidance, helping them navigate the complex terrain of the music business. This willingness to learn from others' experiences has proven to be an invaluable asset in their journey.

One unconventional yet relevant lesson Wavedash has learned is the power of embracing failure. They understood that failure and setbacks are not the end but rather opportunities for growth and improvement. They learned not to be discouraged by rejection or negative feedback but instead use it as a catalyst for self-improvement. By reframing their mindset and viewing failures as stepping stones towards success, Wavedash developed resilience and an unwavering determination to continuously push boundaries and evolve their sound.

It's these lessons that have shaped Wavedash into the formidable force they are today. Their ability to learn from their past mistakes has not only allowed them to grow as artists but has also strengthened their bond as a band. These lessons serve as a reminder that embracing failures, prioritizing authenticity, effective communication, time management, and seeking guidance are vital to personal and artistic development.

As aspiring musicians and music lovers, we can all learn from Wavedash's experiences and apply these lessons in our own lives. Learning from past mistakes is not a sign of weakness but a testament to our desire for growth and improvement. Let Wavedash's journey inspire us to embrace our failures, stay true to our artistic vision, communicate openly, manage our time effectively, seek guidance when needed, and most importantly, never stop evolving and learning.

Subsection: Maintaining a Healthy Work-Life Balance

Maintaining a healthy work-life balance is crucial for the members of Wavedash, as the demands of a music career can be intense and overwhelming. In this subsection, we will explore the importance of finding a balance between work and personal life and provide some valuable tips for achieving this equilibrium.

Why Work-Life Balance Matters

Finding a healthy work-life balance is essential for the overall well-being and success of the members of Wavedash. Here's why it matters:

- **Preventing Burnout:** Continuous work without taking time to unwind can lead to burnout, which can negatively impact creativity, productivity, and mental health. It is crucial to prioritize self-care and relaxation to avoid burnout.

- **Enhancing Creativity:** Engaging in activities outside of work, such as spending time with loved ones, pursuing hobbies, or simply taking a break, can stimulate new ideas and boost creativity. Allowing your mind to wander and recharge can ultimately lead to fresh perspectives in your music-making.

- **Maintaining Relationships:** Neglecting personal relationships for the sake of work can create feelings of isolation and loneliness. Building and nurturing connections with family and friends provide emotional support, which is essential for overall happiness and well-being.

- **Improving Mental and Physical Health:** High levels of stress and work-related pressure can take a toll on mental and physical health. Taking time off to relax, exercise, and engage in self-care activities can help reduce stress levels, improve focus, and enhance overall health.

- **Sustaining Longevity:** A healthy work-life balance contributes to longevity and sustainable success in the music industry. By striking a balance between work and personal life, the members of Wavedash can maintain their passion and energy for music over the long term.

Tips for Achieving Work-Life Balance

Achieving a work-life balance requires conscious effort and planning. Here are some practical tips for the members of Wavedash:

1. **Set Clear Boundaries:** Establish clear boundaries between work and personal life. Determine specific working hours and commit to unplugging from work outside of those hours. Communicate these boundaries to bandmates, collaborators, and team members to ensure everyone respects them.

2. **Prioritize Self-Care:** Make self-care a non-negotiable part of your routine. Set aside time for activities that promote relaxation, such as exercise, meditation, reading, or pursuing hobbies. Prioritizing self-care enhances overall well-being and helps manage stress.

3. **Create a Schedule:** Plan your days and weeks in advance to ensure a healthy balance between work and personal life. Allocate time for music production, rehearsals, meetings, but also include downtime, socializing, and personal activities. A well-organized schedule can help you stay focused and reduce the likelihood of overworking.

4. **Delegate and Collaborate:** Recognize that you don't have to do everything yourself. Delegate tasks to bandmates, assistants, or team members to lighten your workload and free up time for personal pursuits. Collaborating with others can also foster creativity and open doors to new opportunities.

5. **Learn to Say No:** It's important to recognize your limits and not take on more than you can handle. Learn to say no to excessive work requests or commitments that may interfere with your work-life balance. Prioritize activities that align with your goals and values.

6. **Create Separation:** Designate separate spaces for work and leisure to create a physical boundary between the two. Having a dedicated workspace can enhance focus and concentration during work hours, while a separate area for relaxation and leisure helps in mentally disconnecting from work.

7. **Communicate and Collaborate with Loved Ones:** Regularly communicate with your loved ones about your schedule, commitments, and the importance of work-life balance. Involve them in decision-making processes to ensure their understanding and support. Collaboration within personal relationships can help strike a healthy balance between work and personal life.

8. **Take Regular Breaks:** Integrate regular breaks into your work schedule. Stepping away from work intermittently helps recharge your mind, increase

productivity, and prevent burnout. Use these breaks to engage in activities that bring you joy or simply to rest and relax.

9. **Embrace Flexibility:** Recognize that work-life balance is not a fixed formula but rather an ongoing process that requires flexibility. Adjust and adapt as circumstances change. Embracing flexibility allows you to maintain equilibrium even in times of unforeseen challenges.

10. **Enjoy the Journey:** Remember to enjoy the journey and celebrate small victories along the way. The music industry can be demanding, but it's essential to find joy in the process and savor the milestones you achieve. Take the time to celebrate success and appreciate the progress made.

Unconventional Approach: Mandala Coloring

One unconventional yet effective approach to achieving work-life balance is engaging in the art of mandala coloring. Mandala coloring has gained popularity as a therapeutic practice, known for its calming and meditative effects.

The intricate and symmetrical patterns of mandalas can help shift focus away from work-related stressors and promote relaxation. Coloring mandalas stimulates the creative side of the brain, allowing for a mental break from the demands of the music industry. It can be a simple and enjoyable way to unwind and find balance during leisure time.

Consider incorporating mandala coloring into your self-care routine. Set aside a few moments each day to color a mandala and let your mind wander freely. Allow the vibrant hues and balanced patterns to transport you to a state of tranquility, helping you find the balance you need to thrive both personally and professionally.

Summary

Maintaining a healthy work-life balance is a vital aspect of the members of Wavedash's lives. By preventing burnout, enhancing creativity, maintaining relationships, improving mental and physical health, and sustaining longevity, finding equilibrium between work and personal life is key to their overall happiness and success.

Remember, creating a work-life balance requires setting boundaries, prioritizing self-care, scheduling effectively, delegating tasks, learning to say no, creating separation, communicating with loved ones, taking regular breaks, embracing flexibility, and enjoying the journey. And if you're looking for something unconventional, try the calming, meditative practice of mandala coloring.

By prioritizing work-life balance, the members of Wavedash can continue to create their music passionately, build meaningful connections, and leave a lasting impact on the music world.

Section 3: Milestones and Celebrations

Subsection: Chart-Topping Hits and Industry Accolades

When it comes to the music industry, there's nothing quite as thrilling as having a song climb to the top of the charts. It's a testament to an artist's talent and the impact their music has on listeners. For Wavedash, the journey to chart-topping hits and industry accolades has been a rollercoaster ride of hard work, experimentation, and unwavering passion.

The Rise to the Top

Wavedash burst onto the scene with their debut single, "Bang," which quickly gained traction and became a fan favorite. Its infectious beats and catchy melodies propelled the track up the charts, putting Wavedash on the radar of music lovers around the world. The success of "Bang" paved the way for subsequent chart-toppers, solidifying Wavedash's position as a force to be reckoned with in the electronic dance music (EDM) scene.

Exploring New Heights

Building on the success of "Bang," Wavedash continued to push the boundaries of their sound and experiment with different genres. Their second chart-topping hit, "Stallions," showcased their ability to seamlessly blend elements of dubstep, trap, and future bass, creating a unique sonic experience that resonated with fans. The explosive drops and intricate production in "Stallions" hooked listeners and propelled it to the top of the charts.

Collaborations that Soar

In addition to their solo success, Wavedash has collaborated with some of the biggest names in the music industry, resulting in chart-topping tracks that showcase their versatility and ability to adapt to different styles. One such collaboration, "Gravity" featuring NGHTMRE, showcased their talent for combining heavy basslines with melodic elements, resulting in a track that dominated the charts and garnered widespread acclaim.

Industry Accolades and Recognition

Wavedash's chart-topping hits have not gone unnoticed by the industry. Their innovative sound and ability to captivate audiences have earned them numerous accolades, including multiple nominations for the Electronic Music Awards. Their unique blend of genres, intricate production, and electrifying performances have solidified their reputation as trailblazers in the EDM scene.

Unconventional Tactics and Chart Success

Breaking into the music industry is no easy feat, but Wavedash's chart-topping hits have proven that unconventional tactics can lead to success. By actively engaging with their fans on social media, collaborating with artists from different genres, and continuously exploring new sounds, Wavedash has managed to carve out a distinct niche for themselves in the EDM landscape.

Navigating the Challenges of Chart Success

While chart success is undoubtedly a cause for celebration, it also presents its own set of challenges. With heightened expectations and pressure to replicate their hits, Wavedash has had to navigate the delicate balance between staying true to their artistry and meeting commercial demands. Through it all, they have remained committed to pushing their creative boundaries and delivering music that resonates with their fans.

An Enduring Legacy

Wavedash's chart-topping hits and industry accolades have cemented their place in music history. Their ability to create music that transcends genres and captivates audiences has left an indelible mark on the EDM scene. As they continue to evolve and explore new musical territories, the legacy of their chart-topping hits will undoubtedly inspire future generations of artists to push the boundaries of what's possible.

In conclusion, Wavedash's journey to chart-topping hits and industry accolades is a testament to their talent, perseverance, and willingness to push the boundaries of their sound. Their ability to captivate audiences and break through the noise of the music industry has earned them the admiration of fans and industry professionals alike. With an enduring legacy, Wavedash continues to shape the EDM landscape and inspire artists to reach new heights.

Subsection: Memorable Festival Performances

The electrifying energy of Wavedash's live performances is truly a sight to behold. From the moment they step on stage to the last beats of their set, they never fail to captivate the audience with their infectious enthusiasm and skill. Over the years, the band has graced some of the biggest stages in the world, delivering unforgettable performances at countless music festivals. In this subsection, we will take a closer look at some of their most memorable festival moments.

Epic Stage Designs and Visual Spectacles

One of the factors that sets Wavedash apart from other acts is their commitment to delivering an immersive and visually stunning experience. Their performances are a feast for the senses, with intricate stage designs and mind-bending visual effects. At festivals like Electric Daisy Carnival (EDC) and Tomorrowland, they have raised the bar by incorporating stunning LED light displays, pyrotechnics, and even mind-blowing holograms. The fusion of their music with these visual spectacles creates an otherworldly atmosphere that leaves the audience in awe.

Unforgettable Collaborative Performances

Wavedash's festival performances also provide them with the opportunity to collaborate with other artists and push the boundaries of their sound. From surprise guest appearances to planned collaborations, they have shared the stage with some of the biggest names in the industry. Imagine the excitement when they joined forces with electronic music legends like Skrillex and Diplo at Ultra Music Festival, or when they brought out live instruments to perform alongside renowned musicians at Coachella. These collaborative performances elevate their already electrifying sets to new heights and create truly unforgettable moments.

Connecting with the Crowd

One of the most remarkable aspects of Wavedash's festival performances is their ability to connect with the audience on a personal level. Despite the massive crowds, they manage to create an intimate and inclusive atmosphere, making every member of the audience feel like part of the experience. Through interactive moments, engaging stage banter, and genuine interactions, they ensure that everyone feels seen and heard. Whether it's a small underground festival or a large-scale event, their performances are known for their authenticity and the genuine connection they establish with their fans.

Surprise and Spontaneity

In addition to their meticulously planned sets, Wavedash thrives on embracing the unexpected. They love surprising their fans with unexpected transitions, unique remixes, and unreleased tracks during their festival performances. These spontaneous moments not only keep the audience on their toes but also demonstrate their versatility as artists. It's not uncommon to witness impromptu performances by special guests or witness the band experimenting with new sounds and styles right there on stage. This element of surprise adds an extra layer of excitement to their festival performances, making each one a unique experience.

Festival Hacks and Survival Tips

Attending music festivals can be an overwhelming experience, especially for first-timers. However, with their extensive festival experience, Wavedash has some valuable tips to share. From staying hydrated and wearing comfortable shoes to planning your schedule and discovering hidden gems, they provide practical advice to ensure that festival-goers have the best possible experience. They even go the extra mile by sharing festival hacks like portable phone chargers, earplugs, and even fashionable yet functional festival attire. These tips and tricks can make a world of difference in making the most out of the festival experience.

Example: The Unforgettable Bonnaroo Performance

One festival performance that stands out in Wavedash's career is their set at the iconic Bonnaroo Music and Arts Festival. Taking the stage at the legendary Which Stage, the band delivered an awe-inspiring performance that had the crowd in a frenzy. With a setlist that spanned their entire discography, they showcased their versatility and ability to seamlessly blend genres. The stage design featured an array of vibrant neon lights and mesmerizing visuals that perfectly complemented their energetic beats.

Halfway through their set, Wavedash surprised the audience by bringing out a surprise guest, the Grammy-winning rapper Kendrick Lamar. The crowd erupted with excitement as Kendrick joined them on stage for an unforgettable collaboration. Together, they performed a jaw-dropping mashup of Wavedash's hit single "Bang" and Kendrick's chart-topping track "Humble." The fusion of their distinct styles and the undeniable chemistry between them created a once-in-a-lifetime moment that will forever be etched in the minds of those who witnessed it.

As the sun began to set, Wavedash closed their set with their anthemic track "Stargazing." The crowd joined in unison, singing along to every word, filling the air with an indescribable energy. As they bid farewell, the band thanked the audience for their unwavering support and promised to return with more music.

The Bonnaroo Music and Arts Festival performance was a defining moment in Wavedash's career. It showcased their ability to command a massive stage, connect with a diverse crowd, and create an unforgettable festival experience. Their performance serves as a testament to the band's talent, showmanship, and unwavering passion for their craft.

In conclusion, Wavedash's festival performances are a testament to their exceptional artistry and ability to captivate audiences on a global scale. Through their epic stage designs, unforgettable collaborations, genuine connections with the crowd, surprise and spontaneity, and invaluable festival tips, Wavedash continues to leave their mark on the festival circuit. Their performances embody the spirit of celebration, unity, and the power of music to create unforgettable moments that last a lifetime.

Subsection: Reflecting on their Journey and Future Goals

As Wavedash takes a moment to reflect on their incredible journey so far, they can't help but feel a sense of awe and gratitude. From humble beginnings to becoming a force to be reckoned with in the electronic music scene, their path has been filled with both triumphs and challenges. Looking back, they appreciate how far they've come and are excited about what the future holds.

One of the key aspects of their journey that Wavedash reflects upon is the importance of perseverance and staying true to their artistic vision. They remember the early days when they had to work hard to distinguish themselves from the crowd. It wasn't always easy, but they never compromised on their unique sound. It was this dedication to their craft that eventually caught the attention of fans and industry professionals alike.

Wavedash acknowledges that their success wouldn't have been possible without the support of their loyal fanbase. They are grateful for the love and encouragement they have received throughout their career. It's the genuine connections they've made with their fans that have fueled their desire to keep creating music that resonates with people on a deep level.

Looking towards the future, Wavedash has big goals and aspirations. They are constantly seeking new ways to push the boundaries of their sound and experiment with different genres. They understand that growth and evolution are integral to staying relevant in the ever-changing music industry. By staying true to themselves while embracing opportunities for artistic exploration, they hope to continue captivating audiences with their music.

In addition to their musical goals, Wavedash also has a deep desire to make a positive impact on the world. They believe that music has the power to bring people together, and they want to use their platform to spread positivity and inspire change. Whether it's supporting charitable causes or using their voice to advocate for social justice, Wavedash recognizes the importance of giving back and making a difference.

While reflecting on their journey, Wavedash understands the importance of maintaining a balanced perspective. They know that challenges may arise, and the road ahead may not always be smooth. However, they are confident in their ability to overcome obstacles and grow stronger as individuals and as a band. They also value the lessons they have learned along the way and the personal growth that has come with it.

In conclusion, as Wavedash reflects on their journey and contemplates their future goals, they are filled with a sense of excitement and determination. They are committed to staying true to their artistic vision, pushing boundaries, and using their platform to make a positive impact. With their unique sound, unwavering passion, and connection with their fans, Wavedash is poised to leave an enduring legacy in the electronic music scene and beyond. The future is bright, and they can't wait to see where their journey takes them next.

So remember, in the words of Wavedash, "Stay true to yourself, embrace the challenges, and let your passion guide you. The journey may be tough at times, but the rewards are worth it. Keep pushing forward and never give up on your dreams."

Subsection: Commemorating Fan Milestones and Achievements

When it comes to success in the music industry, fans play a crucial role. They are the ones who support and uplift artists, helping them achieve milestones and reach heights they never thought possible. In this subsection, we will explore how Wavedash has commemorated fan milestones and achievements, and the significance of their fanbase in their journey.

Showing Appreciation

Wavedash understands the importance of showing appreciation for their fans. They know that their success wouldn't be possible without the unwavering support of their dedicated followers. To commemorate fan milestones and achievements, Wavedash engages in various activities:

- **Fan Contests and Giveaways:** Wavedash hosts contests and giveaways on social media platforms, allowing fans to win exclusive merchandise, concert tickets, meet-and-greet opportunities, and even private studio sessions. These initiatives not only reward fans for their loyalty but also create a sense of excitement and engagement within the fan community.

- **Fan Art and Fan Covers:** Wavedash encourages their fans to express their creativity by sharing fan art and covers of their music. They showcase some of the best submissions on their social media pages and even collaborate with talented fans to create special edition album covers or merchandise featuring the fan art. This not only acknowledges the talent and dedication of their fans but also fosters a sense of connection and collaboration.

- **Fan Appreciation Events:** Wavedash organizes fan appreciation events, such as meet-ups or pre-show gatherings, where they can interact with their fans on a more personal level. These events create opportunities for fans to have meaningful conversations with the band members, take photos, and make lasting memories. By dedicating time to their fans, Wavedash shows that they genuinely appreciate the support and love they receive.

Honoring Fan Achievements

Wavedash recognizes that their fans achieve remarkable milestones too, and they take joy in celebrating these accomplishments alongside them. Here are some ways in which they honor the achievements of their fans:

- **Fan Spotlights:** Wavedash shines a spotlight on their fans who have achieved significant milestones related to their music. Whether it's a fan releasing their own EP, hitting a certain number of followers on streaming platforms, or performing live for the first time, Wavedash shares their stories and achievements on their social media channels. This not only gives recognition to their fans but also inspires others in the community to chase their dreams.

- **Personalized Messages:** Wavedash goes the extra mile to acknowledge their fans' achievements by sending personalized messages or shout-outs. Whether it's a graduation, a milestone birthday, or an important life event, the band members take the time to connect with their fans on a personal level and celebrate their special moments. This gesture of recognition and support strengthens the bond between the band and their fans.

- **Collaborations with Fans:** Wavedash actively seeks opportunities to collaborate with their talented fans. Whether it's featuring a fan's vocals in a song, showcasing a fan's remix in their DJ sets, or inviting a fan on stage to perform with them, Wavedash embraces the creativity and skills of their fans. These collaborations not only provide fantastic opportunities for the fans but also allow Wavedash to create unique and memorable experiences for their audience.

The Impact of Fan Commemoration

Commemorating fan milestones and achievements has a profound impact on both Wavedash and their fans. Here are some key aspects of this impact:

- **Fostering a Stronger Fan Community:** By acknowledging and celebrating fan milestones and achievements, Wavedash creates a positive and supportive fan community. Fans feel seen, valued, and connected to the band and to each other. This sense of community strengthens their loyalty and encourages them to actively promote and support Wavedash's music.

+ **Inspiring Others:** When fans witness their peers being recognized and celebrated by their favorite band, it ignites a sense of inspiration and motivation. Seeing others achieve their goals within the fan community encourages fans to pursue their own dreams, whether it's in music or any other field. Wavedash becomes a catalyst for personal growth and success among their fans.

+ **Long-lasting Memories:** Being commemorated by Wavedash creates long-lasting memories for their fans. Whether it's winning a giveaway, having their art featured, or collaborating with the band, these experiences become treasured moments that fans cherish for a lifetime. It strengthens the emotional bond between the fans and the band, creating a lasting connection.

In conclusion, Wavedash understands the importance of their fanbase and actively commemorates fan milestones and achievements. By showing their appreciation, honoring fan accomplishments, and creating a strong fan community, Wavedash establishes a unique relationship with their audience. This not only adds depth and meaning to their music career but also leaves a lasting impact on their fans' lives. After all, it is the fans who make the journey worthwhile.

Subsection: Taking Time to Celebrate Success

In the whirlwind journey of their music career, Wavedash has experienced numerous triumphs and reached impressive milestones. Amidst the demanding nature of the music industry and the constant drive for success, it is essential for the members of Wavedash to take a moment to pause, reflect, and celebrate their achievements. This subsection explores the importance of celebrating success, the ways in which Wavedash has done so, and the impact it has had on their artistic journey.

Recognizing Milestones

Wavedash understands the importance of acknowledging and appreciating their successes. The band members make it a point to celebrate various milestones throughout their career. Whether it's achieving chart-topping hits, receiving industry accolades, or reaching significant fan milestones, Wavedash takes the time to reflect on and honor these achievements.

When their debut album surpassed one million streams, the band hosted an intimate gathering for their fans, expressing their gratitude for the support that made their success possible. They also organize annual "Wavedash Anniversary Parties" to commemorate the release of their breakthrough tracks and albums. These events not only give the band an opportunity to connect with their fans but also serve as a reminder of how far they have come in their artistic journey.

Fostering a Supportive Environment

Celebrating success is not just about recognizing personal achievements; it is also about fostering a supportive and encouraging environment within the band. Wavedash places great importance on celebrating each other's victories, big or small. They understand that the success of one member contributes to the success of the entire band.

After the release of a highly anticipated single, the band gathers to toast their accomplishment, showing genuine excitement for each other's talents and hard work. By celebrating one another's achievements, they foster a sense of unity, camaraderie, and motivation within the group, which in turn contributes to their overall success.

Creating Memorable Experiences

Wavedash understands that celebrating success is not just about acknowledging achievements but also about creating memorable experiences that will stay with them and their fans forever. They go above and beyond in planning unique events and experiences to celebrate their milestones.

For instance, to commemorate their first international tour, Wavedash organized an extravagant concert in their hometown. The show incorporated stunning visual effects, immersive set designs, and surprise guest appearances. This celebration not only highlighted their accomplishment but also created a memorable experience for their fans, giving them a chance to be a part of the band's journey.

Expressing Gratitude

In the whirlwind of success, it can be easy to forget the people who have supported and believed in you along the way. Wavedash is meticulous about expressing gratitude to their dedicated fans, as well as to the collaborators, producers, and industry professionals who have contributed to their success.

They often surprise their fans with personalized notes, exclusive merchandise, or even private meet-and-greets to show their appreciation. Additionally, they make a point to publicly acknowledge and thank their team during award ceremonies and industry events. By expressing gratitude, Wavedash not only strengthens their bond with their supporters but also humbles themselves, recognizing that their success is a collective effort.

Inspiring Others

Celebrating success goes beyond personal satisfaction; it also serves as a source of inspiration for others. Wavedash believes in spreading positivity and using their achievements to motivate aspiring musicians and producers.

They actively share their journey, including both the highs and lows, on social media and through interviews, providing insights into their creative process and the challenges they have faced. They understand that their success story can inspire others to pursue their dreams and overcome obstacles along the way.

An Unconventional Approach: Celebrating Failures

While success is often celebrated, Wavedash takes an unconventional approach by also celebrating their failures. They firmly believe that failures are stepping stones to success and view them as opportunities for growth and learning.

To commemorate a particularly challenging production phase, they hosted a "Failure Fête" where they invited their close friends, supporters, and industry peers to join them in acknowledging the failures they experienced during the creative process. Through this event, they aimed to destigmatize failure and encourage others to embrace it as an essential part of the journey to success.

In conclusion, taking the time to celebrate success is crucial for Wavedash. By recognizing milestones, fostering a supportive environment, creating memorable experiences, expressing gratitude, and inspiring others, they not only honor their achievements but also fuel their future endeavors. Through their unconventional approach of celebrating failures, Wavedash embraces the growth mindset and encourages others to do the same. By celebrating success, Wavedash solidifies their legacy as influential musicians who value the journey as much as the destination.

Chapter 4: The Wavedash Legacy

Section 1: Influence on the Electronic Music Scene

Subsection: Inspiring a New Generation of Producers

Music has always been a powerful medium for connection and expression. Throughout history, there have been artists who have pushed boundaries, challenged traditional norms, and inspired a new generation of creators. Wavedash is one such band that has had a profound impact on the electronic music scene, leaving an indelible mark on the hearts and minds of aspiring producers.

Wavedash's innovative sound and fearless approach to music production have captivated audiences worldwide. As pioneers in the genre, they have shown aspiring producers that it is not only possible but also desirable to break away from the mainstream and explore new sonic territories.

One of the key ways in which Wavedash inspires a new generation of producers is by encouraging experimentation. They remind aspiring artists that creativity knows no bounds and that taking risks is an essential part of the artistic process. Through their extensive use of unconventional sounds, intricate synthesizer layering, and unexpected rhythmic patterns, Wavedash demonstrates that music production is as much about pushing limits as it is about technical proficiency.

But inspiring producers goes beyond just musical experimentation; Wavedash also emphasizes the importance of artistic authenticity. In a world where trends come and go, they encourage aspiring producers to stay true to their unique sound and vision. By refusing to conform to industry pressure, Wavedash shows that artistry comes from within and should not be compromised for the sake of commercial success.

Wavedash's collaborative spirit is another aspect that continues to inspire aspiring producers. They have worked with industry giants and fellow producers across a wide range of genres, embracing the idea that collaboration can lead to extraordinary creative opportunities. Through their collaborations, Wavedash demonstrates that by working together, artists can bring out the best in each other and create something truly groundbreaking.

Furthermore, Wavedash's dedication to mentoring and supporting emerging talent has made a significant impact on the electronic music community. They actively seek out opportunities to share their knowledge and experiences with aspiring producers, offering masterclasses, workshops, and online tutorials. By sharing their production techniques, creative processes, and industry insights, Wavedash empowers the next generation of producers to navigate the ever-changing landscape of the music industry.

In an age where technology has made music production more accessible than ever, Wavedash not only inspires producers with their music but also with their use of cutting-edge tools and techniques. They push the boundaries of what is possible in electronic music production, constantly experimenting with new technologies and software. From utilizing advanced sound design techniques to incorporating innovative mixing and mastering approaches, Wavedash showcases the endless possibilities that technology offers to shape and define their unique sound.

To further support and engage with aspiring producers, Wavedash actively encourages them to submit remixes and participate in contests. By providing platforms for emerging talent to showcase their skills, Wavedash not only gives them the opportunity to gain exposure but also offers invaluable feedback and mentorship. This collaborative and inclusive approach fosters a sense of community and support among producers, further inspiring them to pursue their dreams and push their creative boundaries.

To summarize, Wavedash's impact on inspiring a new generation of producers is multi-faceted. Through their emphasis on experimentation, authenticity, collaboration, mentorship, and embracing technology, they empower aspiring producers to find their own unique voice and challenge the status quo. As they continue to pave the way for innovative and boundary-pushing music, Wavedash's legacy will undoubtedly inspire generations of producers to come, shaping the future of the electronic music scene.

Subsection: Shaping the Sound of EDM

The sound of Electronic Dance Music (EDM) is a pulsating force that moves bodies and ignites dance floors around the world. Within this diverse and ever-evolving genre, Wavedash has emerged as a trailblazing force, leaving an indelible mark on the EDM landscape. In this subsection, we will explore how Wavedash has shaped the sound of EDM, pushing boundaries, and redefining what is possible within the genre.

It is impossible to talk about the influence of Wavedash without acknowledging their mastery of sound design. One of the key pillars that have propelled them to the forefront of the EDM scene is their ability to create unique, innovative, and captivating sounds that captivate listeners. Wavedash's meticulous attention to detail combined with their fearlessness to experiment with new sonic textures has allowed them to craft a signature sound that is instantly recognizable.

To understand their impact on shaping the sound of EDM, we need to delve into the techniques they employ to create their distinctive sonic palette. Wavedash is known for pushing the boundaries of sound design by incorporating elements from various musical genres and seamlessly fusing them together. They draw inspiration from diverse influences such as rock, hip-hop, and classical music, infusing their compositions with unexpected and intriguing sonic surprises.

One technique that Wavedash has perfected is the art of using unique and unconventional sound sources. Rather than relying solely on synthesizers and traditional instruments, Wavedash harnesses the power of everyday objects and field recordings to add depth and character to their tracks. For example, they may use the sound of a slamming door, a running faucet, or even the rustling of leaves to create intriguing percussive elements or atmospheric textures. This experimental approach to sound design sets them apart from their contemporaries and adds a refreshing layer of authenticity to their music.

Another aspect of Wavedash's sound that has shaped the EDM scene is their deft manipulation of rhythm. They have a meticulous understanding of how rhythm can be the driving force behind a track, captivating the listener and making them move. Wavedash effortlessly combines intricate syncopated patterns, complex polyrhythms, and unexpected time signatures to create a rhythmic tapestry that keeps audiences on their toes. They are masters of timing, seamlessly transitioning between fast-paced high-energy sections and slower, atmospheric interludes, creating a dynamic and ever-evolving sonic journey.

Wavedash's impact on the sound of EDM extends beyond their studio productions. Their electrifying live performances have set a new standard for EDM shows. Incorporating live instruments, improvisation, and intricate mixing techniques, Wavedash injects a raw and organic energy into their live sets. This interplay between studio productions and live performances allows them to elevate their sound to new heights, creating a truly immersive experience for their audience.

To fully grasp their influence, it is important to note that Wavedash's sound is not only limited to their own productions. Collaborations with other artists, both within the EDM realm and beyond, have allowed them to expand their sonic horizons and leave an indelible mark on various genres. By infusing their distinctive sound into these collaborations, they have expanded the boundaries of EDM and influenced other artists to push their creative limits.

In conclusion, Wavedash's role in shaping the sound of EDM cannot be overstated. Through their innovative sound design, mastery of rhythm, and boundary-pushing collaborations, they have redefined what is possible within the genre. Their ability to seamlessly blend diverse influences and experiment with unconventional sound sources has allowed them to carve out a unique sonic identity. Wavedash's impact on the EDM landscape will continue to resonate for years to come, inspiring a new generation of producers and pushing the boundaries of electronic music.

Subsection: Leaving a Lasting Impact on the Industry

Wavedash, with their innovative sounds and genre-defying music, has undoubtedly left a lasting impact on the electronic music industry. Through their unique approach to production and their ability to push boundaries, they have not only shaped the sound of EDM but have also inspired a new generation of producers.

One of the ways in which Wavedash has made a significant impact is through their experimental and boundary-pushing music. They have constantly pushed the limits of what is possible within the electronic music genre. From their early releases to their more recent tracks, they have consistently delivered fresh and exciting sounds that keep listeners on their toes. By incorporating unconventional elements and blending different genres, they have created a distinctive style that sets them apart from their peers.

An example of their boundary-pushing approach can be heard in their track "Bang". This song combines heavy bass drops with intricate melodies and unexpected sound design. It pushes the boundaries of what is typically considered "acceptable" within the electronic music scene and challenges listeners to expand their horizons.

In addition to their sonic experimentation, Wavedash has also been influential in shaping the production techniques used in EDM. Their meticulous attention to detail and dedication to honing their craft has set a new standard for production quality within the industry. Producers and aspiring artists alike look to Wavedash for inspiration and guidance on how to create a polished and professional sound.

For example, their track "Stallions" showcases their skillful production techniques. The song seamlessly blends complex sound design, intricate drum patterns, and carefully crafted transitions to create a cohesive and powerful listening experience. This attention to detail and commitment to excellence has not only elevated their own music but has also influenced other producers to strive for the same level of professionalism and precision in their work.

Beyond their musical contributions, Wavedash has also made a significant impact through their collaborations and involvement in the EDM community. They have worked with some of the biggest names in the industry, including NGHTMRE and SLANDER, and have brought their unique sound to collaborations that have been met with critical acclaim.

One notable collaboration is their track "Grave" with NGHTMRE. This collaboration brought together the distinct styles of both artists, resulting in a powerful and dynamic track that showcases their individual strengths. Through collaborations like this, Wavedash has not only expanded their own reach to new audiences but has also helped to bridge the gap between different sub-genres within the electronic music community.

In addition to their musical collaborations, Wavedash has also actively engaged with their fanbase and the EDM community through social media and live performances. They have built a strong and dedicated following who are eager to support them at festivals and shows around the world. By connecting directly with their fans and creating a sense of community, Wavedash has fostered an environment of inclusivity and positivity within the EDM scene.

An unconventional yet effective approach that Wavedash has taken to leave a lasting impact is through their philanthropic efforts. They have used their platform and success to give back to their community and support charitable causes. From organizing benefit concerts to donating a percentage of their profits to various organizations, Wavedash has shown a commitment to making a positive difference in the world beyond their music.

For example, they partnered with a local music education program to provide scholarships for aspiring young musicians. By investing in the next generation of artists, Wavedash is ensuring a continued legacy of innovative music and creativity in the industry.

In summary, Wavedash has left a lasting impact on the electronic music industry through their boundary-pushing approach to production, their influence on other producers, their collaborations with industry giants, their engagement with the fanbase, and their philanthropic efforts. Their unique sound and dedication to excellence have not only shaped the sound of EDM but have also inspired a new generation of artists to push the boundaries of what is possible within the genre. As their legacy continues to evolve, their impact on the industry will be felt for years to come.

Subsection: Their Influence on Future EDM Trends

Wavedash has undoubtedly had a profound influence on the future trends of Electronic Dance Music (EDM). Their unique sound and boundary-pushing approach have set the stage for the evolution of the genre. In this subsection, we will explore how their music, production style, and collaborations have shaped the direction of EDM.

Exploring New Sounds and Genres

Wavedash's fearless exploration of new sounds and genres has been instrumental in pushing the boundaries of EDM. They have introduced elements of rock, hip-hop, and experimental electronic music into their tracks, creating a fusion that has captivated audiences worldwide. By infusing diverse influences into their music, Wavedash has inspired other producers to step outside their comfort zones and experiment with different genres. This willingness to take risks has opened doors to new and exciting possibilities within EDM.

Reviving Old-School Production Techniques

While electronic music is known for its use of cutting-edge technology, Wavedash has shown a deep appreciation for old-school production techniques. They have incorporated analog synthesizers, vintage drum machines, and other hardware into their production process, giving their music a distinct warmth and texture. This fusion of old and new has not only brought a fresh perspective to EDM but also inspired a resurgence in interest in classic production methods. Aspiring producers are now exploring the sonic possibilities offered by vintage gear, contributing to a richer and more diverse EDM landscape.

The Rise of Future Bass

One of the most significant contributions of Wavedash to future EDM trends is the popularization of future bass. This subgenre, characterized by its melodic and emotive nature, has gained massive popularity in recent years. Wavedash's innovative approach to sound design, incorporating lush and ethereal synths with heavy basslines, has become synonymous with the future bass sound. Their tracks, like "Bang" and "Starstruck," have become anthems in the genre, inspiring countless producers to experiment with this style. As a result, future bass has become an integral part of the EDM landscape, dominating festival stages and radio airwaves.

Pushing the Boundaries of Production Techniques

Wavedash's commitment to pushing the boundaries of production techniques has had a profound impact on the future of EDM. Their intricate sound design and attention to detail have set a new standard for production excellence. By utilizing advanced synthesis methods, complex sampling techniques, and innovative effects processing, they have expanded the sonic possibilities within EDM. As a result, producers around the world have embraced more intricate and detailed production techniques, enhancing the overall quality of electronic music.

Collaborations with Diverse Artists

Wavedash's collaborations with diverse artists have played a significant role in shaping future EDM trends. By working with musicians from various genres, they have bridged the gap between EDM and other musical styles. Collaborations with artists such as Illenium, QUIX, and SLANDER have resulted in genre-blurring tracks that have resonated with a wide audience. These collaborations have not only expanded the sonic palette of EDM but have also opened up new avenues for artistic exploration and cross-genre experimentation.

Incorporating Live Instruments into EDM

In addition to their forward-thinking production techniques, Wavedash has also been instrumental in incorporating live instruments into EDM. They have seamlessly blended electronic elements with live guitar, drums, and other instruments, creating a unique and dynamic sound. By bringing live instrumentation to the forefront of their performances, Wavedash has challenged the perception that EDM is solely a studio-based genre. Their fusion of electronic and live elements has inspired other producers to incorporate live instruments into their music, adding a newfound depth and organic feel to EDM tracks.

In conclusion, Wavedash's influence on future EDM trends cannot be understated. Through their boundary-pushing sound, incorporation of diverse genres, and innovative production techniques, they have paved the way for the evolution of electronic music. Their impact will continue to shape the future of EDM, inspiring producers and musicians to push the boundaries of creativity and explore new sonic territories. Wavedash's contribution to the genre's growth and development is a testament to their artistic vision and unwavering dedication to pushing the envelope in EDM.

Subsection: The Wavedash Sound in Popular Culture

The distinctive sound of Wavedash has made a significant impact on popular culture, permeating various aspects of society beyond the realm of electronic dance music (EDM). Their unique blend of genres, innovative production techniques, and captivating melodies have garnered them a dedicated fan base and caught the attention of music enthusiasts across the globe. In this subsection, we will explore the influence that Wavedash has had on popular culture, from mainstream media to advertising campaigns, fashion, and art.

Mainstream Media

Wavedash's music has found its way into the mainstream media, making appearances in movies, television shows, and commercials. Their energetic and anthemic tracks have been featured in action-packed movie trailers, adding an extra layer of intensity and excitement to the visuals. The combination of Wavedash's high-energy sound and cinematic imagery creates an immersive experience for the audience, elevating the impact of the visuals.

In television shows, Wavedash's tracks have been used to heighten the drama and suspense in pivotal scenes. Whether it's a climactic moment in a thrilling series or a high-octane sports event, their music has the power to intensify the emotions and keep viewers at the edge of their seats. This integration of Wavedash's sound in mainstream media not only showcases their versatility but also introduces their music to a wider audience.

Advertising and Fashion

The distinct sound of Wavedash has also found its way into the advertising world. Their dynamic and imaginative tracks have been used in commercials for various products and services, ranging from sports brands to tech companies. Wavedash's music adds a sense of energy, modernity, and innovation to these campaigns, resonating with their target demographics.

Moreover, Wavedash's influence extends beyond just their music. Their unique fashion sense has also made waves in popular culture. Known for their eclectic style and bold fashion choices, the members of Wavedash have become trendsetters, inspiring fans and fashion enthusiasts alike. Their aesthetic has been featured in fashion editorials, and they have collaborated with renowned fashion designers to create limited edition merchandise and apparel, which further solidifies their impact on popular culture.

Artistic Collaborations

Wavedash's ability to create immersive and atmospheric soundscapes has caught the attention of artists from various disciplines. Their collaborations with visual artists, dancers, and filmmakers have resulted in multimedia experiences that push the boundaries of artistry. By combining their music with captivating visuals, choreography, and storytelling, Wavedash has created multidimensional art forms that engage the senses and evoke a range of emotions.

One notable collaboration involved an interactive art installation where Wavedash's tracks were used as the soundtrack to a visually stunning exhibit. Visitors could navigate through different rooms, each representing a different dimension of their sound, immersing themselves in a sensory experience that blurred the lines between music, art, and technology. This innovative approach to collaboration showcases Wavedash's commitment to pushing artistic boundaries and creating unique experiences for their audience.

Educational Initiatives

Beyond engaging with popular culture, Wavedash has also found ways to make an impact on education. Their music has been incorporated into music production programs and workshops, inspiring a new generation of producers and musicians. By sharing their production techniques, insights, and industry experiences, Wavedash empowers aspiring artists to explore their creative potential and find their own unique sound.

Through partnerships with educational institutions and online platforms, Wavedash provides resources, tutorials, and mentoring opportunities for emerging artists. This commitment to supporting the growth of the music community ensures that their influence extends beyond their own success, cultivating a vibrant and diverse creative landscape.

The Wavedash Sound as a Cultural Phenomenon

The distinct sound of Wavedash has become more than just music. It has become a cultural phenomenon that represents innovation, boundary-pushing, and artistic expression. Their ability to captivate audiences with their infectious melodies, intricate sound design, and powerful performances has solidified their status as one of the most influential acts in the electronic music scene.

The impact that Wavedash has had on popular culture is a testament to the transformative power of music. Their ability to transcend boundaries and captivate audiences from different backgrounds is a testament to the universality and accessibility of their sound. As they continue to evolve and explore new musical territories, the Wavedash sound will undoubtedly continue to shape the future of popular culture, leaving an indelible mark on the creative landscape.

In conclusion, the Wavedash sound has made a significant impact on popular culture, from mainstream media to advertising campaigns, fashion, and art. Their unique blend of genres, innovative production techniques, and captivating melodies have allowed them to transcend the boundaries of the electronic music scene and capture the attention of a diverse range of audiences. Through their music, fashion, collaborations, and educational initiatives, Wavedash has become a cultural force, pushing artistic boundaries and inspiring future generations of artists.

Section 2: Wavedash's Philanthropy and Social Impact

Subsection: Giving Back to their Community

Giving back to their community has always been a core value for Wavedash. From the beginning, they understood the importance of supporting and uplifting the people and places that shaped their musical journey. In this subsection, we will explore Wavedash's philanthropic efforts and their impact on the community.

One of the ways Wavedash gives back is through charity concerts and fundraising events. They organize and participate in benefit concerts, with proceeds going towards charitable organizations and causes they are passionate about. For example, they have performed at events supporting mental health awareness, environmental conservation, and music education.

To further their impact, Wavedash also collaborates with local organizations on community outreach projects. They actively seek opportunities to work with schools, community centers, and non-profit organizations to inspire and nurture the next generation of musicians. Wavedash believes that everyone should have access to music education, regardless of their background or financial means. They support programs that provide instruments, lessons, and mentorship to aspiring musicians who may not have the resources to pursue their passion.

Wavedash's commitment to giving back extends beyond their music-related initiatives. They understand that social issues are interconnected, and they use their platform to raise awareness and advocate for positive change. They actively engage with their fans through social media campaigns, encouraging them to be part of the solution. For example, they have mobilized their fanbase to support local food banks, participate in beach clean-ups, and volunteer at shelters.

Additionally, Wavedash allocates a portion of their earnings towards charitable donations. They have established their own philanthropic foundation, which distributes funds to various causes they believe in. This includes supporting organizations that focus on mental health, environmental sustainability, and social justice. They prioritize transparency and regularly share updates with their fanbase about the impact of their donations.

Wavedash recognizes the importance of giving back not only to their immediate community but also to the global community. They actively seek collaborations with international organizations, artists, and musicians to support causes on a global scale. By leveraging their platform and influence, they are able to amplify their impact and inspire positive change beyond their local reach.

As an example of their international philanthropic efforts, Wavedash recently partnered with a non-profit organization to provide clean drinking water to communities in developing countries. They organized fundraising campaigns and used their performances as a platform to raise awareness about the global water crisis. Their fans rallied behind the cause, and together, they were able to fund the installation of several water filtration systems, improving the quality of life for thousands of people.

Wavedash's commitment to giving back is not only altruistic but also serves as an inspiration to their fans and the music community at large. They believe that artists have a responsibility to use their platform for positive change and to address societal issues. Through their philanthropic efforts, Wavedash demonstrates that music can be a catalyst for transformation, and that artists have the power to make a difference in the world.

In summary, Wavedash is dedicated to giving back to their community in meaningful and impactful ways. Through charity concerts, collaborations with local organizations, fundraising events, and their own philanthropic foundation, they are actively working towards making a positive change in the world. By using their platform and influence, they inspire their fans to get involved and be part of the solution. Wavedash's commitment to giving back is a testament to their belief in the power of music to create positive change and leave a lasting impact on society.

Subsection: Using Their Platform for Social Change

In addition to their musical talents, Wavedash is renowned for using their platform to promote social change and make a positive impact on the world. Through their music, performances, and philanthropic efforts, the band members strive to address important issues and inspire their fans to take action. Let's dive into how Wavedash leverages their influence to create a better world.

Elevating Social Issues Through Music

Wavedash recognizes the power of music as a tool for raising awareness and fostering dialogue around social issues. Through their lyrics and melodies, they tackle topics such as mental health, inequality, and environmental sustainability. By incorporating meaningful messages into their songs, they encourage their listeners to reflect on these issues and engage in conversations that lead to societal change.

One example of their impactful music is the song "Breaking Barriers," which sheds light on the struggles faced by marginalized communities. The lyrics address systemic oppression and advocate for equality and justice. This thought-provoking track earned widespread praise for its powerful message and engagement with important social issues.

Collaborations with Non-Profit Organizations

Wavedash believes in the power of collaboration to amplify their impact. They actively seek partnerships with non-profit organizations that align with their values and goals. By teaming up with these organizations, Wavedash can maximize their reach and resources to effect change on a larger scale.

For instance, they collaborated with the Climate Change Alliance, a global environmental organization, to raise awareness about the pressing issue of climate change. Together, they organized a series of fundraising concerts, with proceeds going towards initiatives that promote sustainability and carbon reduction. By using their music as a catalyst for change, Wavedash not only raises funds but also inspires their fans to take sustainable actions in their own lives.

Engaging Fans in Social Impact Initiatives

Wavedash recognizes the power of their fan base and actively involves their fans in social impact initiatives. They have created online platforms where fans can connect, share ideas, and take part in collective action. Through these platforms, Wavedash encourages their fans to contribute to causes they are passionate about and provides resources and opportunities for them to make a difference.

One initiative called "Wavedash Warriors" encourages fans to engage in volunteer work and community service. Wavedash partners with local organizations and coordinates volunteer opportunities for their fans to contribute their time and skills to meaningful causes. By inspiring their fans to take action, Wavedash creates a ripple effect, fostering a community of socially conscious individuals dedicated to positive change.

Empowering Underrepresented Voices

Wavedash is committed to amplifying the voices of underrepresented communities. They actively promote inclusion and diversity within the music industry and beyond. Through their collaborations and performances, they create opportunities for talented artists from marginalized backgrounds to showcase their work and gain recognition.

In addition, Wavedash uses their influence to champion gender equality in the STEM fields, launching scholarship programs to support young women pursuing careers in technology and music production. By providing resources and mentorship, they aim to empower these aspiring artists and bridge the gender gap in the industry.

Continuing the Legacy

As Wavedash's influence grows, so does their commitment to making a difference. They understand that social change is an ongoing process, and they are dedicated to continuing their efforts in the years to come. Wavedash plans to expand their social impact initiatives globally, partnering with organizations worldwide to create lasting change on a larger scale.

Moreover, the band is exploring new ways to merge art and activism through multimedia projects that combine music, film, and technology. They believe that by embracing innovative approaches, they can engage audiences in unique and impactful ways, furthering their mission of driving social change through their art.

In conclusion, Wavedash uses their music, collaborations, and platform to make a positive impact on society. By addressing social issues, partnering with non-profit organizations, engaging fans in social impact initiatives, empowering underrepresented voices, and planning for the future, the band members strive to leave a lasting legacy of positive change. Through their work, they inspire not only music lovers but also a generation of individuals who believe in using their talents to create a better world.

Subsection: Building a Positive Legacy

Building a positive legacy is not just about achieving success in the music industry; it is also about making a significant impact on society and leaving a lasting positive impression on the world. Wavedash understands the importance of using their platform for social change and has been actively involved in various philanthropic endeavors throughout their career. In this subsection, we will explore their philanthropic efforts, their dedication to social impact, and how they have been building a positive legacy beyond their music.

Giving Back to their Community

Wavedash is deeply committed to giving back to their community and supporting local initiatives. They understand the power of music to bring people together and make a difference. One of their key initiatives is organizing charity events and fundraisers to support causes close to their hearts. They actively collaborate with other artists and organizations to create unique experiences that raise awareness and funds for various charitable organizations. By harnessing the power of their music and their fanbase, they have been able to make a significant impact in their community.

Using Their Platform for Social Change

Wavedash recognizes that they have a platform that can reach a wide audience and influence change. They utilize their social media channels to raise awareness about social issues and advocate for positive change. They amplify the voices of marginalized communities and shed light on important social justice causes. By leveraging their influence, they work towards creating a more inclusive and equitable society. Through their authentic and genuine engagement, they inspire their fans to take action and be agents of change themselves.

Building a Positive Legacy

Building a positive legacy is about more than just financial success and fame. It is about leaving a mark on the world that goes beyond the confines of the music industry. Wavedash understands this and consistently takes actions that contribute to a better future. They actively engage with organizations and initiatives that align with their values, from environmental sustainability to mental health awareness.

Support for Charitable Causes

Wavedash shows unwavering support for charitable causes by dedicating a portion of their tour proceeds and merchandise sales to various organizations. They actively collaborate with non-profit entities, aligning their efforts to create a significant impact. By supporting charitable causes, they amplify the work of these organizations, positively affecting the lives of many.

Engaging Fans in Social Impact Initiatives

Wavedash understands that their fans play a crucial role in the success of their philanthropic initiatives. They actively involve their fanbase in social impact projects, encouraging them to participate in fundraising events, volunteer work, and awareness campaigns. By engaging their fans in these initiatives, they create a sense of shared responsibility and inspire their audience to be agents of change in their own communities.

Leaving a Legacy of Inspiration

Wavedash's commitment to building a positive legacy is not limited to their musical achievements. They strive to inspire their fans and future generations of artists to use their talents and platforms for the greater good. Through their actions and dedication to social impact, they set an example for aspiring musicians to prioritize values and impact alongside their artistic pursuits.

In conclusion, Wavedash is not only passionate about their music but also about making a positive difference in the world. By giving back to their community, using their platform for social change, and supporting charitable causes, they are building a legacy that extends beyond their musical accomplishments. Their commitment to social impact inspires their fans and sets a new standard for artists in the industry. Wavedash's true essence lies in their ability to leave the world a better place through their music and their actions.

Subsection: Support for Charitable Causes

In addition to their incredible musical talent, the members of Wavedash have also shown a strong commitment to giving back to their community and using their platform for social change. They understand the importance of using their success and influence to make a positive impact in the world. In this subsection, we will explore the various charitable causes that Wavedash supports and the ways in which they have used their music and platform to raise awareness and provide assistance.

One of the charitable causes that Wavedash is passionate about is mental health. They have openly discussed their personal struggles with mental health and believe that it is crucial to raise awareness and create a supportive environment for those facing similar challenges. Through their music and social media presence, Wavedash has been vocal about the importance of seeking help and finding support systems. They have collaborated with mental health organizations to raise funds and promote resources for those in need. Wavedash has organized benefit concerts and events, with all proceeds going towards mental health initiatives.

Another cause that Wavedash actively supports is environmental conservation. They are passionate about preserving the planet and have used their music and influence to advocate for sustainable practices. Wavedash has participated in environmental campaigns, such as beach cleanups and tree planting initiatives. They have also partnered with organizations focused on protecting endangered species and ecosystems. Through their concerts and social media platforms, Wavedash raises awareness about the impact of human activities on the environment and encourages their fans to take action.

Wavedash understands the importance of education and equal opportunities for all. They have supported initiatives that aim to provide education and resources to underserved communities. Through partnerships with educational organizations, Wavedash has contributed to scholarships and educational programs for disadvantaged students. They have also organized music workshops and mentorship programs, where they share their knowledge and skills with aspiring musicians.

In times of crisis, Wavedash has shown their commitment to providing assistance and support. They have organized benefit concerts and donated a portion of their earnings to organizations helping communities affected by natural disasters, such as hurricanes and earthquakes. Through their music and social media platforms, Wavedash has helped raise funds for emergency relief efforts and spread awareness about the importance of supporting those in need during difficult times.

Wavedash actively engages with their fans to encourage their involvement in charitable causes. They have organized fan-driven fundraising campaigns, where fans are encouraged to donate to a specific cause. Wavedash also actively uses their social media platforms to promote and raise awareness about different charities and their initiatives.

In addition to their support for existing charitable causes, Wavedash has also initiated their own foundation, dedicated to creating positive change in various areas of society. The foundation focuses on supporting local communities, promoting artistic expression, and advocating for social justice. Through their foundation, Wavedash aims to make a long-lasting impact on the world beyond their music.

To encourage their fans to get involved in charitable causes, Wavedash often organizes unique and creative fundraising events. They have hosted charity auctions, where fans can bid on exclusive merchandise, concert tickets, and even opportunities to meet the band. This not only raises funds for the cause but also creates a sense of excitement and community among their fanbase.

Overall, Wavedash's commitment to supporting charitable causes demonstrates their desire to use their music and influence for good. Their efforts to raise awareness, provide support, and make a positive impact in the world serve as an inspiration to their fans and to the music industry as a whole. By supporting various causes and actively engaging with their community, Wavedash has proven that music has the power to bring about positive change. As they continue to evolve and grow as artists, we can expect them to remain dedicated to their philanthropic endeavors and continue their support for charitable causes.

Subsection: Engaging Fans in Social Impact Initiatives

Engaging fans in social impact initiatives is not just about making music; it's about using your platform to make a positive change in the world. Wavedash understands the power they hold as artists and the influence they have over their fans. They are dedicated to making a difference and impacting society beyond the music industry. In this subsection, we will explore how Wavedash engages their fans in social impact initiatives and how they encourage their followers to take action.

One of the primary ways Wavedash engages their fans in social impact initiatives is through their involvement in various charitable causes. They actively seek out partnerships with organizations that align with their values and mission. By supporting such causes, they inspire their fans to get involved and make a difference themselves. Wavedash often collaborates with charitable organizations that focus on issues such as mental health awareness, environmental conservation, and social justice.

To promote these initiatives, Wavedash organizes fundraising events during their tours and performances, where a portion of the proceeds goes directly to the designated charity. They also utilize their social media platforms to raise awareness about important causes and provide resources for their fans to take action. By using their artistry to promote philanthropy, Wavedash encourages their fans to be socially conscious and active agents of change.

Wavedash goes beyond just monetary contributions by actively engaging their fans in hands-on volunteer work. They organize community service projects such as beach cleanups, food drives, and music-related workshops for underprivileged youth. These initiatives provide a unique opportunity for fans to connect with the band members, collaborate with like-minded individuals, and make a tangible impact in their communities.

In addition to their involvement in charitable initiatives, Wavedash takes it a step further by incorporating social impact themes into their music and performances. They believe in the power of storytelling through music to ignite change and inspire their fans. Wavedash often incorporates socially conscious lyrics and themes related to important issues like mental health, inequality, and personal growth.

By addressing these topics through their music, Wavedash not only generates awareness but also fosters meaningful conversations among their fans. They encourage their listeners to reflect on these issues and take action in their own lives. This approach allows Wavedash to connect with their fans on a deeper level, using their music as a catalyst for positive change.

To actively engage their fans, Wavedash encourages fan participation and creates spaces for meaningful dialogue. They organize interactive fan events where attendees can share personal experiences related to social impact initiatives and discuss ideas for creating a better world. These events foster a sense of community and empower fans to see themselves as agents of change.

Moreover, Wavedash leverages their social media platforms to amplify the voices of their fans who are making a difference in their communities. They regularly feature fan stories and initiatives on their channels, providing a platform for individuals to share their efforts and inspire others. This not only builds a stronger bond between the band and their fans but also encourages a ripple effect of positive change.

Wavedash recognizes that engaging fans in social impact initiatives goes beyond just promoting causes. It requires creating a supportive and inclusive community where fans feel empowered to make a difference. They work to foster a sense of belonging among their fan base, promoting a safe environment for open discussions, and providing resources for personal growth and self-improvement.

In conclusion, Wavedash understands the importance of engaging fans in social impact initiatives. Through their involvement in charitable causes, hands-on volunteer work, incorporating social impact themes into their music, and creating spaces for meaningful dialogue, Wavedash encourages their fans to take action and make a positive change in the world. Their commitment to social impact extends beyond the music industry, shaping their legacy as artists who use their platform to inspire and empower others.

Section 3: Artistic Evolution and Future Ventures

Subsection: Exploring New Genres and Sounds

In their constant pursuit of artistic growth and innovation, Wavedash has never been afraid to step out of their comfort zone and explore new genres and sounds. This subsection delves into their journey of pushing musical boundaries and embracing new sonic landscapes.

Embracing Diversity in Genres

Wavedash understands the power of diversity in musical genres and the importance of breaking free from the conventions of a single genre. They believe that true creativity lies in the ability to blend different styles and experiment with unconventional combinations.

One of the ways Wavedash has explored new genres is through collaboration. They have sought out artists from completely different genres, such as hip-hop, rock, and even classical music. By fusing their electronic sound with elements from these diverse genres, Wavedash has been able to create unique and refreshing tracks that defy categorization.

Take their collaboration with a renowned hip-hop artist, for example. Wavedash seamlessly incorporated hip-hop beats and vocals into their signature electronic sound, resulting in a track that bridged the gap between the worlds of EDM and hip-hop. This cross-pollination of genres not only expands the boundaries of their music but also attracts a wider audience with diverse musical preferences.

Experimenting with Soundscapes

Wavedash embraces the limitless possibilities of sound and constantly seeks to create immersive sonic worlds that transport listeners to new dimensions. They excel at experimenting with various soundscapes, crafting intricate layers of melodies, textured rhythms, and atmospheric elements.

In their exploration of new genres and sounds, Wavedash has turned to unconventional sources of inspiration. They draw inspiration from everyday sounds, nature, and even non-musical objects. From the gentle rustling of leaves to the dissonant hum of machinery, Wavedash finds beauty and musical potential in the smallest details of our environment.

By incorporating these unique sounds into their music, Wavedash adds a distinct and organic dimension to their soundscapes. The fusion of these atmospheric elements with their electronic production techniques creates an otherworldly experience for listeners, blurring the boundaries between reality and imagination.

Pushing the Envelope

Wavedash constantly challenges themselves to push the envelope and create music that stands out from the rest. They are unafraid to step into uncharted territories, embracing experimentation as a means of artistic expression.

One way they have pushed the boundaries is by incorporating unconventional instruments and techniques into their compositions. By utilizing instruments not typically associated with EDM, such as the sitar or didgeridoo, Wavedash creates a truly unique sonic palette that sets them apart from their contemporaries.

Moreover, they have embraced innovative production techniques that break traditional norms. For example, they have explored glitch aesthetics by intentionally introducing digital distortions and artifacts into their tracks. This unconventional approach adds a raw and edgy quality to their music, captivating listeners with its unpredictable and ever-evolving nature.

Blurring Genre Lines

Wavedash is known for their ability to blur the lines between different genres, creating a sound that is uniquely their own. By seamlessly blending elements from multiple genres, they transcend traditional genre categorizations and carve out a distinct sonic identity.

Their innovative approach to fusion has led to the birth of new and exciting subgenres within EDM. Drawing inspiration from genres like dubstep, drum and bass, and trance, Wavedash has reinterpreted these styles in their own unique way, injecting fresh energy and ideas into the EDM scene.

This blurring of genre lines has not only made Wavedash's music stand out but has also inspired a new generation of producers to experiment with different genres, further pushing the boundaries of electronic music.

Unconventional Collaboration: The Sound of Nature

In their quest for new sounds and inspirations, Wavedash embarked on an unconventional collaboration with a field recording artist who specializes in capturing natural sounds. The collaboration involved integrating recordings of various natural environments into their music.

These natural soundscapes provided a unique sonic palette for Wavedash to work with. From the mesmerizing melodies of bird chirping to the rhythmic patterns of raindrops hitting the ground, the integration of these sounds added a profound sense of depth and connection to the natural world.

This collaboration not only expanded Wavedash's artistic horizons but also raised awareness about the environment and the need to preserve it. Through their music, Wavedash sought to convey a message of harmony between humans and nature, urging listeners to appreciate the beauty and importance of our natural surroundings.

Exercise: Creating Your Unique Sound

Explore the boundaries of your own musical taste by creating your unique sound. Mix different genres together, experiment with unconventional instruments, and push the limits of traditional production techniques. Embrace the power of collaboration and seek inspiration from unexpected sources. Blend the sounds of nature with electronic elements, or venture into uncharted territories by fusing unexpected genres together. Take risks, trust your instincts, and let your imagination guide you in the pursuit of creating music that truly reflects your artistic vision.

Subsection: Solo Projects and Side Collaborations

Wavedash's journey in the music industry hasn't been limited to their work as a collective. Throughout their career, the members of Wavedash have also pursued solo projects and collaborations outside of the group, showcasing their versatility and individual artistic visions. In this section, we will explore some of their exciting solo endeavors and noteworthy side collaborations.

Arjun Roy: "ARJUN"

Arjun Roy, one of the talented members of Wavedash, has embarked on a solo project under the name "ARJUN." With ARJUN, Roy explores different genres and soundscapes, showcasing his diverse musical talents beyond the realms of electronic music.

One of ARJUN's notable releases is the EP "Eclipse." This project finds Roy delving into experimental electronic sounds, incorporating elements of ambient music and downtempo beats. The EP takes listeners on a journey through atmospheric melodies and intricate sound design, creating a captivating sonic experience. Tracks like "Lunar," with its ethereal textures and haunting vocals, demonstrate Roy's ability to create deeply immersive music that transcends genres.

Roy's solo project allows him to experiment with unconventional production techniques and showcase his skills as a multi-instrumentalist. From incorporating live instrumentation to experimenting with unconventional time signatures, ARJUN's music is a testament to Roy's commitment to pushing boundaries and exploring new sonic territories.

Michael Stone: "SOLSTIS"

Michael Stone, another member of Wavedash, has pursued his musical endeavors under the moniker "SOLSTIS." With SOLSTIS, Stone delves into the world of melodic bass music, infusing vibrant synths, catchy melodies, and powerful vocals into his productions.

One of SOLSTIS' standout releases is the album "Nowhere," a dynamic collection of tracks that showcase Stone's exceptional production skills and knack for crafting infectious melodies. Tracks like "Cataclysm" and "About You" display Stone's ability to balance powerful basslines with emotive melodies, resulting in an uplifting and energetic listening experience.

As SOLSTIS, Stone has also collaborated with other artists in the electronic music scene. His collaboration with Devault on the track "Electricity" is a perfect blend of their individual styles, seamlessly merging Devault's dark and atmospheric soundscapes with Stone's melodic prowess. This collaboration highlights the importance of artistic synergy and the ability to create something unique by combining different creative visions.

Gary Smith: Side Productions and Remixes

Gary Smith, the third member of Wavedash, has also pursued his musical career outside of the group through various side productions and remixes. Smith's solo work encompasses a wide range of electronic music genres, showcasing his versatility as a producer.

One notable side project of Smith is his collaboration with fellow musician Ryan Browne under the name "DirtySnatcha." Their music explores the realms of bass music, with heavy drops, intricate sound design, and infectious rhythms. Tracks like "Wigsplitta" and "Space Out" demonstrate Smith's talent for creating hard-hitting and energetic bass music that is sure to ignite dancefloors.

In addition to side projects, Smith has produced remixes for renowned artists such as Alison Wonderland and Zeds Dead. His remix of Alison Wonderland's

"Happy Place" transforms the original track into a high-energy dancefloor anthem, infusing it with heavy basslines and explosive drops. Smith's remixes showcase his ability to reimagine existing songs and add his unique touch while staying true to the essence of the original tracks.

Exploring New Horizons

While Wavedash's collaboration as a group remains their primary focus, their solo projects and side collaborations allow each member to explore new horizons, experiment with different genres, and showcase their individual artistic visions. These endeavors not only contribute to their personal growth as artists but also bring fresh perspectives and influences back to their work with Wavedash.

In an ever-evolving music landscape, exploring different creative avenues is essential for artists to stay inspired and continue pushing boundaries. Wavedash's willingness to dive into solo projects and side collaborations demonstrates their commitment to artistic growth and their passion for pushing the boundaries of electronic music.

As fans eagerly anticipate new releases and collaborations from Wavedash, their solo projects and side endeavors offer a glimpse into the individual creativity and diverse talents that make up the collective. It's through these explorations that Wavedash continues to shape their sound, contribute to the music industry, and leave a lasting legacy in the EDM scene.

Key Takeaways and Future Prospects

- Members of Wavedash have pursued solo projects and side collaborations outside of the group, showcasing their individual artistic visions and versatility. - Arjun Roy explores different genres and soundscapes with his solo project, ARJUN, experimenting with experimental electronic sounds and ambient music. - Michael Stone, under the name SOLSTIS, delves into melodic bass music, incorporating vibrant synths and catchy melodies into his productions. - Gary Smith, through side projects like DirtySnatcha and remixes, explores bass music and showcases his versatility as a producer. - Solo projects and side collaborations enable members of Wavedash to bring fresh perspectives and influences back to their work as a collective. - As Wavedash continues to evolve, their solo projects and side endeavors contribute to their artistic growth and impact on the electronic music scene.

Subsection: Looking Ahead to the Next Chapter

As Wavedash approaches the next chapter of their music career, they are filled with excitement and anticipation for what lies ahead. With their innovative sound and unique style, they have already made a significant impact on the electronic music scene. But what can we expect from them in the future?

Exploring New Genres and Sounds

Wavedash has never been content with staying within the confines of a single genre. Throughout their journey, they have continuously pushed boundaries and experimented with different sounds. In the next chapter, they plan to continue exploring new genres and expanding their sonic palette.

One area of interest for Wavedash is incorporating elements of hip-hop and R&B into their music. They have always been fascinated by the blending of different genres and are excited to infuse their signature sound with elements from these genres. Through collaborations and creative experimentation, they hope to create a unique fusion that appeals to fans across multiple musical spheres.

Another avenue they are eager to explore is the realm of live instrumentation. While their music is predominantly electronic, they recognize the power and expressiveness of live instruments. They plan to incorporate more live drums, guitars, and other instruments into their productions, adding a new layer of depth and authenticity to their sound.

Solo Projects and Side Collaborations

In addition to their collective work as a band, each member of Wavedash is brimming with individual creative energy. The next chapter will see them embarking on solo projects and side collaborations, allowing them to explore their artistic visions and musical interests in a more personal capacity.

These solo projects will not only showcase the individual talents of each member but will also bring a fresh perspective to their collective work. By branching out and collaborating with artists outside of their immediate circle, they will bring new ideas and influences back to the band, enriching the overall Wavedash sound.

Additionally, these side projects will provide the band members with individual opportunities for growth and self-expression. It will allow them to experiment with different genres, styles, and production techniques, further honing their craft and expanding their creative horizons.

Looking Ahead to the Next Chapter

As Wavedash sets their sights on the next chapter of their career, they are filled with an unwavering determination to continue pushing boundaries and evolving as artists. They have already left an indelible mark on the electronic music scene, but they are far from done.

They envision themselves as pioneers, shaping the sound of electronic music and inspiring future generations of producers.   By consistently challenging themselves and exploring new artistic territories, they hope to leave a lasting impact on the industry.

Wavedash is not just about making music; they are about making a difference. They believe in using their platform to create positive social change and give back to their community. Through philanthropic initiatives and social impact projects, they aim to build a legacy that extends beyond their music.

The next chapter of Wavedash is filled with excitement, creativity, and a commitment to experimentation. They are ready to face new challenges, overcome obstacles, and continue to captivate audiences with their electrifying performances. The journey has only just begun, and the best is yet to come.

Unconventional Wisdom

In this ever-changing music landscape, it is crucial for artists to adapt and evolve. Wavedash understands the importance of staying true to their creative instincts while also embracing new possibilities. They know that by stepping out of their comfort zone and exploring unfamiliar territories, they can unlock untapped potential and discover new dimensions of their artistry.

One unconventional yet vital piece of wisdom they have learned is the power of collaboration. By working with artists from different genres and backgrounds, they can gain fresh perspectives and push the boundaries of their own sound. This approach not only keeps their music exciting and relevant but also opens up new avenues for growth and exploration.

Another unconventional practice they swear by is taking breaks and allowing themselves time to recharge. In an industry that often glorifies a non-stop hustle, Wavedash recognizes the importance of self-care and maintaining a healthy work-life balance. By taking the time to rest and rejuvenate, they can approach their music with renewed energy and creativity.

Summary

As Wavedash looks ahead to the next chapter of their musical journey, they are eager to explore new genres, incorporate live instrumentation, and embark on solo projects and side collaborations. They aim to shape the sound of electronic music, while also making a positive social impact through philanthropy and advocacy. With a commitment to pushing boundaries, embracing collaboration, and taking breaks, Wavedash is poised to leave an enduring legacy in the music industry. The future is bright, and the possibilities are limitless for this dynamic band.

In the realm of creative expression, possibilities are limitless. Artists often find inspiration in various mediums to expand their artistic horizons, and Wavedash is no exception. While their primary focus lies in music production and live performances, they have also ventured into other artistic mediums, seeking new avenues to express their unique vision. In this subsection, we will explore Wavedash's exploration of other artistic realms and the impact it has had on their creative journey.

One of the artistic mediums that Wavedash has delved into is visual art. They recognize the power of visuals in enhancing the overall experience of their music. Drawing on their background in graphic design, the members of Wavedash have sought to create or collaborate on visual content that complements their music. They believe that incorporating captivating visuals amplifies the emotional impact of their performances, creating a multisensory experience for their audience.

To achieve this, Wavedash has collaborated with talented visual artists to bring their music to life on stage. Through the careful interplay of light, color, and motion, they aim to create immersive visual landscapes that resonate with their musical compositions. The synchronized visuals enhance the narrative of their performances, adding depth and dimension to their live shows.

In addition to live performances, Wavedash has also explored the creation of music videos. They recognize the power of storytelling through visual narratives and the potential of music videos to captivate and engage listeners. By combining their musical expertise with visual storytelling, they create audio-visual experiences that enrich the meaning behind their songs.

Wavedash's foray into other artistic mediums has allowed them to exercise their creativity in new ways. Experimenting with visual art has not only expanded their artistic range but has also deepened their understanding of how music and visuals can harmonize to create a truly immersive experience. This cross-pollination of art forms has fueled their ability to connect with their audience on a more profound level.

Additionally, Wavedash has embraced the realm of fashion as an opportunity for artistic expression. They believe that fashion can be a powerful tool for self-expression and a means to visually communicate their music's energy and aesthetic. Collaborating with fashion designers, they have created unique stage outfits that embody their music's vibrant spirit.

By exploring other artistic mediums, Wavedash has also fostered collaborations with artists from diverse backgrounds. This interplay of different artistic perspectives has led to exciting and unexpected creative synergies, further enriching their creative process. These collaborations have allowed them to experiment with new sounds, styles, and genres, pushing the boundaries of their musical expression.

While their primary focus remains on music, Wavedash's exploration of other artistic mediums demonstrates their willingness to embrace multidimensionality and evolve as artists. This expansion into visual art and fashion allows them to manifest their music's essence through different means, giving them the freedom to explore new creative territories.

In conclusion, Wavedash's journey into other artistic mediums has been an enriching experience. Their ventures into visual art and fashion have not only expanded their creative horizons but have also enhanced their music and live performances. By intertwining music, visuals, and fashion, Wavedash continues to evolve as artists, pushing the boundaries of their creative expression. This commitment to multidimensionality ensures that their artistic legacy will resonate for years to come, leaving a lasting impact on the intersection of music and art.

Subsection: Future Goals and Aspirations

As Wavedash continues to make waves in the world of electronic music, they have set their sights on a bright and exciting future. With their unique blend of experimental sounds and infectious beats, the band has already achieved great success and recognition. However, they are not content to rest on their laurels. In this subsection, we will explore Wavedash's future goals and aspirations, as they strive to push boundaries and leave a lasting legacy in the music industry.

One of Wavedash's primary goals is to continue exploring new genres and sounds. The band members firmly believe in the power of experimentation and innovation. They are eager to delve into uncharted musical territories, testing the limits of their creativity and craftsmanship. By incorporating influences from a wide range of genres, they hope to create a sound that is truly unique and groundbreaking.

In order to achieve this, Wavedash plans to embark on solo projects and side collaborations. While their collective work as a band is undoubtedly impressive, they recognize the value of individual artistic expression. Each member of

Wavedash possesses their own distinct musical sensibilities and preferences. By working on side projects, they can fully explore and showcase their individual styles, while still maintaining a strong connection to the band. These solo ventures will not only challenge and inspire the members of Wavedash but also provide fans with a diverse array of musical experiences.

Looking ahead to the next chapter of their careers, Wavedash aspires to expand into other artistic mediums. They recognize that music is just one avenue for creative expression. With their dynamic and imaginative approach to music production, it is only natural for them to explore other art forms. From visual arts to filmmaking, they aim to push the boundaries of their creativity and bring their unique perspective to a variety of artistic endeavors. By collaborating with other artists from different disciplines, they hope to create multimedia experiences that captivate and inspire audiences.

Of course, as they venture into new territories, Wavedash remains committed to their core values and the electronic music scene that launched their careers. They understand the importance of staying connected to their roots and the community that has supported them. They plan to continue championing the electronic music genre, inspiring a new generation of producers and shaping the sound of EDM.

In addition to their artistic pursuits, Wavedash is also dedicated to making a positive social impact. They understand the power of music to bring people together and effect change. Therefore, they plan to use their platform to advocate for causes close to their hearts, supporting charitable initiatives and spreading awareness about important social issues. By engaging their fans in these efforts, they hope to empower others to make a difference and create a better world.

Looking towards the future, Wavedash envisions a world where their music transcends borders and boundaries. They aspire to take their exhilarating live performances to international stages, sharing their vibrant sound with audiences from around the globe. They hope to collaborate with artists from different cultures and backgrounds, fusing their unique styles to create a truly global musical experience.

As Wavedash continues to pursue their goals and aspirations, they remain grounded and focused on personal growth and resilience. They understand the challenges that come with success in the music industry and are committed to maintaining a healthy work-life balance. They prioritize their mental and emotional well-being, seeking support when needed and actively spreading awareness about the importance of mental health.

In conclusion, the future of Wavedash is filled with exciting possibilities and endless potential. Their unwavering passion for music and dedication to pushing boundaries will undoubtedly drive them to create groundbreaking music and art.

By remaining true to their artistic vision, embracing collaboration, and striving for personal growth, Wavedash is poised to leave a lasting impact on the music industry and inspire generations to come. The journey continues, and the world eagerly awaits the next chapter of Wavedash's extraordinary musical odyssey.

Conclusion

Section 1: Lessons Learned and Final Thoughts

Subsection: Growing as Artists and Individuals

As artists and individuals, the members of Wavedash have undergone a remarkable journey of growth, both in their musical careers and in their personal lives. This section explores the various challenges they have faced and the valuable lessons they have learned along the way.

One of the most significant aspects of their growth has been their commitment to pushing boundaries and constantly evolving their sound. Wavedash has never been afraid to experiment with new genres and explore unconventional sounds. This willingness to take risks and embrace change has allowed them to stay ahead of the curve and maintain their relevance in an ever-evolving music industry.

In their early years, Wavedash faced many creative challenges as they worked to refine their sound and find their artistic identity. They spent countless hours in the studio experimenting with different production techniques and sound design. Through trial and error, they discovered what worked for them and what didn't, allowing them to carve out their unique sonic signature.

Collaborations have also played a key role in their growth as artists. By working with industry giants and cross-genre collaborators, Wavedash has been able to expand their musical horizons and learn from the best. These collaborations have not only helped them refine their craft but have also exposed them to new perspectives and ideas, further fueling their creative growth.

Balancing creativity with commercial success has been another challenge Wavedash has faced. As their popularity grew, they had to navigate the delicate balance of creating music that resonated with their audience while staying true to their artistic vision. This process required them to make tough decisions and sometimes take risks, but ultimately it has allowed them to achieve a level of success without compromising their integrity.

But growth isn't just about the music. It's also about personal development and maintaining a healthy work-life balance. Wavedash has learned the importance of taking care of themselves both physically and mentally. They have sought support and sought help when needed, recognizing that their well-being is paramount to their artistic success.

To spread awareness and advocate for mental health, Wavedash has used their platform to start conversations and break down stigmas surrounding mental health issues. They have shared their own experiences, showing vulnerability and proving that seeking help is a sign of strength, not weakness. Their openness has resonated with fans and created a community of support and understanding.

Throughout their journey, Wavedash has also recognized the importance of learning from past mistakes. They have embraced these experiences as opportunities for growth and have used them as stepping stones towards their future success. They have shown resilience in the face of adversity and have emerged stronger and wiser as a result.

Looking ahead, Wavedash has exciting prospects and ambitious goals. They are exploring new genres and sounds, eager to push their creative boundaries even further. They also have plans for solo projects and side collaborations, allowing them to further diversify their artistic output. Their passion and dedication to their craft ensure that they will continue to evolve as artists and individuals, leaving an indelible mark on the music world.

In conclusion, the members of Wavedash have grown immensely as both artists and individuals. Through their commitment to pushing boundaries, embracing change, and learning from their experiences, they have become true trailblazers in the electronic dance music scene. Their journey is a testament to the power of perseverance, creativity, and personal growth. As they continue to evolve and explore new artistic ventures, their influence and legacy are sure to endure for years to come.

Subsection: Wavedash's Impact on the Music World

Wavedash, the iconic electronic music group, has left an undeniable impact on the music world. Their unique sound, innovative approach to production, and dynamic live performances have influenced countless artists and helped shape the landscape of EDM.

One of the key ways that Wavedash has made an impact is through their distinct sound. Their music blends elements from various genres, fusing together heavy basslines, intricate melodies, and powerful drops. This sonic fusion has inspired a new generation of producers who seek to push boundaries and experiment with different styles.

By constantly pushing the envelope, Wavedash has been able to shape the sound of EDM itself. Their use of intricate sound design, unconventional song structures, and experimental production techniques has challenged the status quo and encouraged others to think outside the box. As a result, the EDM genre has become more diverse and dynamic.

Wavedash's impact can also be seen in their collaborations with other artists. By working with industry giants and crossing over into different genres, they have helped bridge the gap between EDM and mainstream music. These collaborations have allowed their unique sound to reach a wider audience and have blurred the lines between different musical styles.

In addition to their musical contributions, Wavedash has also made an impact through their live performances. Known for their energetic stage presence, captivating visuals, and immersive production design, their shows create a truly unforgettable experience for their fans. This emphasis on creating a multisensory experience has inspired other artists to elevate their live performances and push the boundaries of what is possible on stage.

Beyond their musical and performance prowess, Wavedash has also made a significant impact through their philanthropic efforts and social advocacy. They have used their platform to raise awareness about important social issues and have actively supported charitable causes. By engaging their fans in social impact initiatives, they have created a sense of community and inspired others to use their voices and resources for positive change.

Looking ahead, Wavedash's impact on the music world is likely to endure. Their innovative approach to music production, their ability to push boundaries and think outside the box, and their unwavering commitment to artistic integrity will continue to inspire future generations of musicians and shape the trajectory of electronic music.

In conclusion, Wavedash has made a significant impact on the music world through their distinct sound, innovative production techniques, dynamic live performances, and philanthropic efforts. Their influence can be seen in the evolution of EDM, the cross-genre collaborations they have undertaken, and their ability to inspire others to think creatively and make a positive impact. Wavedash's legacy is one that will continue to resonate for years to come, leaving an indelible mark on the music industry.

Subsection: The Enduring Spirit of Wavedash

The enduring spirit of Wavedash can be traced back to their unwavering passion for music and their relentless pursuit of artistic excellence. From their humble beginnings to their current status as electronic music superstars, Wavedash has consistently pushed boundaries, challenged norms, and inspired millions of fans around the world. In this subsection, we will explore the key factors that have contributed to the enduring spirit of this remarkable band.

At the heart of Wavedash's enduring spirit is their commitment to authenticity and innovation. Since their formation, they have always stayed true to their unique style and sound, refusing to conform to industry expectations or trends. This unwavering dedication to their artistic vision has set them apart from their peers and garnered them a loyal and passionate fanbase.

In addition to their commitment to authenticity, Wavedash has consistently strived to push the boundaries of electronic music. They have continually experimented with new sounds, blending genres, and incorporating unconventional elements into their music. This fearless approach to creativity has allowed them to evolve their sound and stay ahead of the curve, ensuring that their music remains fresh and relevant.

Furthermore, Wavedash's enduring spirit can be attributed to their relentless work ethic and commitment to their craft. They have always approached their music with a level of professionalism and dedication that is unparalleled. Countless hours spent in the studio, experimenting with sounds, refining their production skills, and perfecting their compositions have been instrumental in shaping their unique sound and catapulting them to success.

Another factor that has contributed to Wavedash's enduring spirit is their genuine connection with their fans. Despite their rapid rise to fame, they have always made an effort to engage with their audience on a personal level. From fan meet-and-greets to social media interactions, they have built a community around their music—a community that is fueled by a shared love for their art and an appreciation for their humble and down-to-earth nature.

Wavedash's endurance can also be attributed to their resilience in the face of challenges. They have navigated the ups and downs of the music industry with grace and determination, refusing to let setbacks define them. Their ability to overcome obstacles, both personal and professional, has not only strengthened their bond as a band but has also inspired others to persevere in their own pursuits.

Additionally, Wavedash's enduring spirit can be seen in their commitment to using their platform for social change. They have leveraged their influence to raise awareness for important causes and give back to their community. Their involvement in charitable initiatives and their dedication to making a positive impact on the world is a testament to their enduring spirit and their desire to leave a lasting legacy.

In conclusion, the enduring spirit of Wavedash can be attributed to their commitment to authenticity, innovation, and hard work. Their fearless approach to creativity, their connection with their fans, their resilience in the face of challenges, and their dedication to making a positive impact on the world set them apart as a band that transcends the boundaries of electronic music. As they continue to push the boundaries of their art and inspire others along the way, the enduring spirit of Wavedash will surely continue to resonate for years to come.

Chapter 4: The Wavedash Legacy

Section 1: Influence on the Electronic Music Scene

Wavedash has undoubtedly left an indelible mark on the electronic music scene. Their innovative sound and boundary-pushing approach have inspired a new generation of producers and shaped the very fabric of EDM. In this section, we will explore the profound influence that Wavedash has had on the electronic music landscape.

Subsection: Inspiring a New Generation of Producers

Wavedash's groundbreaking music has inspired countless aspiring producers to explore new sonic territories and experiment with unconventional sounds. Their willingness to take risks and challenge traditional genre norms has shown emerging artists that it is possible to break free from established conventions and pave their own artistic path.

One of the ways in which Wavedash has inspired a new generation of producers is through their signature sound design. Their intricate and complex soundscapes, characterized by haunting melodies, heavy basslines, and intricate rhythms, have become a benchmark for aspiring producers looking to elevate their own music production skills.

Furthermore, Wavedash's ability to seamlessly blend genres has opened up new possibilities for producers looking to explore the intersections of different musical styles. By fusing elements of dubstep, trap, and drum and bass, among others, they have demonstrated that electronic music is not bound by rigid genre boundaries, but rather a limitless medium for artistic expression.

Wavedash's impact on the electronic music scene extends beyond their music production skills. Through their collaborations and mentorship of emerging artists, they have actively nurtured the next generation of talent. By sharing their knowledge and experiences, they have empowered budding producers to find their own voice and make their mark on the industry.

Subsection: Shaping the Sound of EDM

Wavedash's unique sound has had a profound impact on the evolution of EDM. Their incorporation of heavy basslines, intricate rhythms, and unconventional sound design techniques has redefined the possibilities of what electronic music can sound like.

Their influence can be seen in the works of numerous artists who have adopted elements of Wavedash's style into their own music. From the rising stars of dubstep to established names in the industry, the impact of Wavedash's sound can be heard reverberating throughout the electronic music scene.

Moreover, Wavedash's willingness to experiment with different musical styles and push the boundaries of genre conventions has influenced the broader EDM landscape. By challenging established norms and persistently exploring new sonic territories, they have encouraged other artists to step outside of their comfort zones and embrace innovation.

Subsection: Leaving a Lasting Impact on the Industry

Wavedash's impact on the electronic music industry extends far beyond their music. By consistently delivering high-quality releases, captivating performances, and innovative music videos, they have set new standards of excellence within the industry.

Their commitment to professionalism, artistic integrity, and innovation has earned them the respect and admiration of their peers. They have become trailblazers within the industry, inspiring other artists to strive for greatness and pushing the boundaries of what is possible in electronic music.

Furthermore, Wavedash's success has demonstrated that it is possible for independent artists to achieve mainstream recognition and commercial success without compromising their artistic vision. Their story has served as a source of inspiration for countless aspiring musicians who dream of carving their own path in the music industry.

Subsection: Their Influence on Future EDM Trends

Wavedash's impact on the electronic music scene is not confined to the present; it extends into the future as well. Their groundbreaking music and innovative approach to production have set the stage for future trends in EDM.

By constantly pushing boundaries and exploring new sonic territories, Wavedash has paved the way for the emergence of new sub-genres and styles within electronic music. The influence of their sound can be seen in the works of up-and-coming artists who are continuing to push the envelope and redefine the genre.

Additionally, Wavedash's commitment to authenticity and innovation has challenged the notion that electronic music is purely focused on dancefloor hits. Their music has demonstrated that electronic music can be a deeply emotional and introspective art form, capable of evoking a wide range of emotions beyond just making people dance.

In conclusion, Wavedash's enduring spirit has had a profound impact on the electronic music scene. Their commitment to authenticity, innovation, and pushing boundaries has inspired a new generation of producers, shaped the sound of EDM, left a lasting impact on the industry, and influenced future EDM trends. As their legacy continues to unfold, the impact of Wavedash on the electronic music landscape will undoubtedly persist, shaping the direction of the genre for years to come.

Subsection: Continuing Influence and Legacy

As Wavedash continues to make waves in the world of electronic music, their influence and legacy have become increasingly apparent. With their groundbreaking sound, creative collaborations, and dedication to their craft, Wavedash has left an indelible mark on the industry and inspired a new generation of producers and musicians.

One of the most significant ways in which Wavedash has maintained their influence is through their unique sound. From their early experimental music exploration to their refined production skills, the trio has consistently pushed the boundaries of electronic music. Their signature blend of heavy bass, intricate melodies, and captivating rhythms has become a benchmark for aspiring producers worldwide.

Wavedash's distinct sound has not only shaped the EDM genre but has also influenced the sound of popular music as a whole. Their fusion of electronic elements with other genres, such as hip-hop and rock, has created a new sonic landscape that has been emulated by many artists. Their innovative approach to sound design and production techniques has set them apart from their peers and continues to inspire others to think outside the box.

In addition to their impact on the sound of music, Wavedash's collaborative efforts have further solidified their influence and legacy. Their collaborations with industry giants have not only resulted in chart-topping hits but have also pushed the boundaries of creativity in the EDM world. By teaming up with artists from different genres and backgrounds, Wavedash has created a unique fusion of styles that has resonated with diverse audiences.

Their ability to balance artistic integrity with commercial success is a testament to their exceptional talent and vision. Wavedash's collaborative performances, both in the studio and on stage, have showcased their ability to seamlessly merge different musical styles into a cohesive and innovative sound. Their cross-genre collaborations have brought new listeners to the EDM scene and have expanded the reach of electronic music beyond its traditional audience.

Beyond their music, Wavedash has also made a significant impact through their philanthropic endeavors and social impact initiatives. Recognizing the importance of giving back to their community, the trio has actively engaged in charitable causes and used their platform to raise awareness for social issues. Their dedication to spreading positivity and advocating for change has endeared them to their fans and further solidified their legacy as more than just musicians.

Looking ahead to the future, Wavedash is poised to continue their artistic evolution and venture into new territories. Their willingness to explore new genres and sounds demonstrates their commitment to pushing the boundaries of their creativity. Whether through solo projects, side collaborations, or expansion into other artistic mediums, Wavedash is sure to leave their mark on the music industry for years to come.

As the music world evolves and new trends emerge, Wavedash's enduring spirit will remain a source of inspiration for both established and aspiring artists. Their unique sound, innovative collaborations, and commitment to making a positive impact have elevated them to become true pioneers in the EDM scene. Wavedash's legacy will continue to shape the future of electronic music and leave an indelible imprint on the industry for generations to come.

In the words of Wavedash themselves, "We never want to settle for complacency. We always want to push ourselves, explore new territories, and continue to evolve as artists. Our aim is to leave a lasting impact on the industry and inspire others to follow their passion and create music that is true to themselves. The journey is far from over, and we're excited to see what the future holds."

And so, the legacy of Wavedash lives on, inspiring new generations of producers, challenging the status quo, and pushing the boundaries of what electronic music can be. As their influence continues to reverberate through the industry, one thing is certain - Wavedash has forever changed the landscape of electronic music and their legacy will remain etched in the annals of musical history.

Subsection: Future Outlook and Exciting Prospects

The future of Wavedash is as bright and promising as ever. As they continue to push the boundaries of electronic music, they are constantly evolving and exploring new sounds and genres. With their unique style and distinctive sound, Wavedash has carved out a special place for themselves in the music world. In this subsection, we will delve into some of the exciting prospects that lie ahead for this talented trio.

Exploring New Musical Directions

Wavedash has always been known for their innovative approach to music production, constantly pushing the boundaries of what is considered "normal" in the electronic music scene. As they look to the future, they are eager to explore new musical directions and experiment with different genres.

One exciting prospect on the horizon for Wavedash is their interest in incorporating live instruments into their performances. While electronic music is primarily created using synthesizers and digital instruments, Wavedash is keen on blending traditional elements with their signature futuristic sound. They have expressed their desire to work with talented instrumentalists and bring a new dimension to their music by incorporating live drums, guitars, and other instruments into their tracks.

Additionally, Wavedash is planning to explore other genres outside of electronic music. They have expressed interest in collaborating with artists from different musical backgrounds, such as hip-hop, pop, and rock. This cross-genre experimentation will undoubtedly result in refreshing and unexpected collaborations that will captivate their audience and push the boundaries of electronic music even further.

Shaping the Future of Music Production

As technology continues to advance at an unprecedented rate, so does the realm of music production. Wavedash has always been at the forefront of embracing new technology and harnessing its power to create groundbreaking sounds. They firmly believe that the future of music production lies in constantly adapting to emerging technologies.

One aspect that Wavedash is particularly excited about is the integration of artificial intelligence (AI) in music production. They see immense potential in utilizing AI algorithms to generate unique melodies, harmonies, and even entire tracks. By leveraging AI, Wavedash hopes to enhance their creativity and expand their sonic palette, allowing them to produce music that is truly one-of-a-kind.

Furthermore, Wavedash is actively exploring the possibilities of virtual reality (VR) and augmented reality (AR) in their live performances. They envision a future where concert-goers can immerse themselves in a completely interactive and visually stunning experience. Through the use of VR headsets and AR overlays, they aim to create a multisensory journey that blurs the line between reality and music, leaving their fans in awe.

Continued Musical Collaborations

Collaborations have always been an integral part of Wavedash's journey, and they have no intention of slowing down in the future. They recognize that collaborating with other talented artists not only expands their musical horizons but also allows them to tap into new audiences and fan bases.

In addition to collaborating with established electronic music superstars, Wavedash also aims to nurture and support emerging talent. They believe in the power of mentorship and giving back to the music community. By collaborating with up-and-coming artists, they hope to provide a platform for them to showcase their skills and help them navigate the ever-changing music industry.

Expanding Their Artistic Endeavors

Wavedash is not limited to the confines of the music industry. They have expressed a keen interest in expanding into other artistic mediums, such as visual arts and fashion. They see these creative outlets as opportunities to further express their artistic vision and connect with their fans on a deeper level.

For instance, Wavedash envisions collaborating with visual artists to create immersive visual experiences that accompany their music. Whether it's through mesmerizing music videos or interactive installations, they aim to create a holistic sensory experience that goes beyond just the music.

Furthermore, fashion plays a significant role in Wavedash's identity. They have a unique fashion sense that complements their music and stage presence. In the future, they plan to collaborate with fashion designers and create their own line of merchandise that reflects their futuristic aesthetic.

Future Goals and Aspirations

With their meteoric rise in the electronic music scene, Wavedash has set their sights on achieving even greater heights. They have several goals and aspirations that they hope to accomplish in the coming years.

One of their primary goals is to embark on a world tour and perform in renowned venues and festivals across the globe. They want to share their music with fans from different cultures and connect with people on a global scale. The energy and passion they bring to their live performances are unparalleled, and they are eager to bring their exhilarating shows to fans around the world.

Additionally, Wavedash has expressed their desire to use their platform to make a positive impact on society. They are committed to giving back to their community and supporting charitable causes. Whether it's through benefit concerts, collaborations with nonprofit organizations, or actively spreading awareness about social issues, they aim to be a force for good in the world.

In conclusion, the future outlook for Wavedash is filled with endless possibilities and exciting prospects. Their commitment to pushing boundaries, embracing new technologies, and exploring different musical directions will undoubtedly lead to groundbreaking innovations in the world of electronic music. With their distinctive sound and forward-thinking approach, Wavedash is poised to leave an indelible mark on the music industry and captivate audiences for years to come.

Index

9 781779 693167